AF272986

This is a first edition of 2,000
and is numbered:

0012 ✳

Julian Mash is a graduate of the University of East Anglia's MA programme. He lived and worked in Notting Hill for over a decade, half of which was spent working at the Travel Bookshop, a local institution and the inspiration for the bookshop in the film *Notting Hill*. He is the author of *Portobello Road: Lives of a Neighbourhood* and was the recipient of the RSL Jerwood Award for Non-Fiction. His writing has appeared in the *Telegraph*, *Evening Standard* and *Q* magazine amongst others. He is the literary programmer for End of the Road Festival and works for the publisher Unbound. He lives in London with his partner and their two children.

NOTTING HILL
A Walking Guide

—

Julian Mash

Notting Hill Editions

Published in 2018 by Notting Hill Editions Ltd
Mirefoot, Burneside, Kendal, Cumbria LA8 9AB

Original design by FLOK Design, Berlin, Germany
Cover design by Plain Creative, Kendal
Cover illustration by Owain Kirby
Typeset by CB editions, London

Printed and bound
by Memminger MedienCentrum, Memmingen, Germany

The right of Julian Mash to be identified as the author of this work
has been asserted in accordance with Section 77 of the Copyright,
Designs and Patents Act 1998

Maps and Photographs by Joseph Turnbull
Japanese Translation by Tomoko Alderson
Editor: Rosie Heys
Copy Editor: Emma Dickens

This book is sold subject to the condition that it shall not, by way of
trade or otherwise, be lent, resold, hired out or otherwise circulated
without the publisher's prior consent in any form of binding or cover
other than that in which it is published and without a similar condition
including this condition being imposed on the subsequent purchaser.

A CIP record for this book is available from the British Library

ISBN 978-1-910749-944

www.nottinghilleditions.com

For my parents: John and Annie

Contents

Kim Kremer

– Preface –

N otting Hill Editions was founded by my father Tom Kremer in 2011. Tom began his commercial life in Notting Hill when he founded a toy invention company named Seven Towns, in Kensington Park Road in 1963. The company licensed both his own inventions and those of other creatives – Rubik's Cube was one of his greatest successes (a puzzle he championed despite being told it 'would never work'). Seven Towns continues to flourish today in its studios off Westbourne Grove.

Tom was born in Transylvania, and emigrated to Britain in the 1950s. He met my Scottish mother Lady Alison Balfour at Edinburgh University. There was an unlikely but immediate attraction between them: Alison used to say that she knew instantly that this strange, scruffy Hungarian would be a significant person in her life. Their relationship was frowned upon but they moved in together, unmarried and broke, and eventually settled in Notting Hill – a remarkably open-minded place even in the Fifties. They bought a run-down house in St James's Gardens which had no running water, and rented a room to a professional gambler who paid the rent irregularly from his winnings. There, in that rambling, tall house, they brought up my brother, my sister and me. Our neighbours were an Irish laundress and an Italian restaurateur. The rag-and-bone man regularly drove by in his horse-drawn cart, calling for scrap.

Alison worked as a journalist and food writer, and Tom took odd jobs until he hatched Seven Towns in a moment of epiphany. Notting Hill was, and still is, a culturally rich and interesting area, a fertile place for new initiatives. Even as an eccentric Translyvanian Jew, Tom always felt at home and formed a strong and life-long attachment to the area.

After a successful business career in toy invention Tom decided, at the age of eighty, to fulfill his passion for literature. In a fast-moving digital world, Tom's aim was to nurture the slower art of deep conversation and ideas-mongering. He set out to revive the art of the essay, and to create exceptionally beautiful books that would be cherished. He named the venture Notting Hill Editions because he felt that this iconic name would resonate wherever it was heard. The company began its life at Newcombe House on Notting Hill Gate.

Tom asked me to join Notting Hill Editions in 2014, and we worked together until his death in 2017. Had he lived to see this book he would have said, 'But of course! There is nowhere in the *world* like Notting Hill.'

Julian Mash's book is a walk through the cultural, social and architectural history of this remarkable part of London. You can take your imagination for a stroll from the comfort of an armchair or put on your boots and tread the pavements, as you follow in the footsteps of Notting Hill's iconic and revolutionary residents. Welcome to Notting Hill, and happy walking!

– Introduction –

W alking is the best way to explore and make sense of a city. There is no barrier to entry. No ticket is required. Select some comfortable shoes; choose a route or area; and away you go. Whenever I visit an unfamiliar city I try to walk as much as I can, sometimes with no clear destination in mind. This can lead to some startling discoveries that would never have happened had I simply gone from A to B.

I have lived in London for the past fifteen years, over a decade of which has been spent in Notting Hill, and I have found walking to be the best way to unlock the secrets of the neighbourhood. It is not just about what you will see when you walk, but who you will meet. I have made lifelong friends and connections by walking around the Portobello Road market, chatting to stallholders and seeing familiar faces in the local coffee shops.

When you live in a city it is all too easy to become stuck in old routines, wedded to certain routes that you walk over and over again. And with the rise of the smartphone many of us are cocooned in a digital world as we walk, listening to music or podcasts as we stroll, unaware of, or uninterested in, what lies around us. Think of this walking guide to Notting Hill as an antidote to the iPhone – designed to put you back in touch with your surroundings. In her book *Wanderlust: A History of Walking*, Rebecca Solnit describes how the activity should be '. . . a state in which the mind, the body, and the world are aligned, as though they were three characters finally in conversation together, three notes suddenly making a chord. Walking allows us to be in our bodies and in the world without being made busy by them. It leaves us free to think without being wholly lost in our thoughts.'

Notting Hill is perfectly suited to being enjoyed on foot and these four walks are designed to give you a feel for its rich and diverse history. The neighbourhood has changed dramatically over the last sixty years, transformed from a shabby, run-down district into one of the most desirable and expensive postcodes in the city. The four walks contained here are arranged thematically – think of them as snapshots of the recent past. You will learn about the origins of the Notting Hill Carnival that takes place every August Bank Holiday weekend; you will walk the length of the famous Portobello Road Market, discovering how it has evolved over the years and meeting some of its longest-standing traders; you will visit some of the neighbourhood's iconic buildings and learn about the lives of the people who lived in them; and you will be introduced to the wealth of culture the area has spawned in film, music and literature – from Hawkwind to Hugh Grant.

Waves of gentrification have altered the neighbourhood greatly over recent years, but despite these changes, it retains a unique character and charm that the influx of money cannot eradicate. I agree with the words of the protagonist in G. K. Chesterton's locally set novel *The Napoleon of Notting Hill*: 'There has never been anything in the world absolutely like Notting Hill. There will never be anything quite like it to the crack of doom. I cannot believe anything but that God loved it as He must surely love anything that is itself and unreplaceable.'

– The Market –

1. Barham Antiques, 111 Portobello Road. **2**. Virgin Records HQ, Vernon Yard Mews. **3**. The Portobello Estate.
4. The Red Lion Arcade, 165–169 Portobello Road.
5. Junction of Talbot Road and Blenheim Crescent – the main venue for street entertainment and political demonstrations in the early 20th century. **6**. Canopy under the Westway, vintage market Friday/Saturday. **7**. Acklam Village Market.
8. I Was Lord Kitchener's Valet, 293 Portobello Road.
9. George's Portobello Fish Bar, 329 Portobello Road.

Walking the length of Portobello Road from Notting Hill Gate in the south, to Golborne Road in the north is one of the best ways to explore the neighbourhood. There is nothing more enjoyable than to spend a day navigating the market stalls that appear, as if by magic, overnight and populate this stretch of West London. Fridays and Saturdays are traditionally the busiest days for the market, though Sunday is increasingly popular. Each section of the street has its own distinct character and speciality – from vintage clothes underneath the Westway canopy, to street food on Golborne Road; and the arcades between Westbourne Grove and Elgin Crescent, which sell every kind of collectable and antique imaginable. Portobello is known the world over as one of the biggest antique markets in the UK, with over a thousand dealers attracting 100,000 visitors a week. Consequently, it can take a while to walk anywhere on market days, so be prepared for the crowds and expect a slow stroll rather than a brisk walk. Whilst Portobello Road has seen some major changes over the last ten years, losing some of its best-loved independent shops, and witnessing the arrival of High Street chains, it retains a raffish, bohemian charm that marks it out as a unique corner of London.

So, let's get started. Make your way to **Alice's Antiques at 86 Portobello Road**. Alice's is one of the oldest antique shops in the neighbourhood, dating from a time when most of this stretch was dominated

Alice's Antiques featured heavily in the recent
Paddington film

by the trade. Those that remain, including Barham
Antiques at 111 and Judy Fox at 81, offer an insight
into how things used to be – the owners are all friends,
helping one another out with deliveries and sending
customers to whichever one best suits their needs. The
antique trade sprang up here in the post-war era when
rents were cheap and many traders started out with
market stalls before graduating to shops. That was the
case with **Barham Antiques at 111 Portobello**. Today
it is run by Michael Barham, whose father started trading from a market stall in the late 1940s after he was
demobbed from the army. Things went well and he
bought the building, a former Welsh dairy, in the early
1950s and there they have remained ever since. If you
venture inside you will find beautiful wooden boxes,
alongside tea caddies and whisky glasses.

Continue walking north down Portobello, cross the junction with Westbourne Grove and keep an eye, and an ear, out for buskers. Busking has long been a feature on Portobello with many now famous singers having first thrown down their hat and strapped on a guitar here. From Dave Brock of Hawkwind fame, to more recent pop singers the Sugar Sisters, who can still be heard serenading shoppers with their sweet harmonies on occasional Saturdays.

Pause outside Vernon Yard mews at **119 Portobello Road**. Portobello Road was of course named after Admiral Edward Vernon who took Porto Belo in central America (now in Panama) from the Spanish in the 1739 War of Jenkins' Ear, with the street taking its name from his great victory. In more recent times Richard Branson's Virgin Records label was based out of number **2–4 Vernon Yard** in the 1970s and 1980s when records like Mike Oldfield's *Tubular Bells* and the Sex Pistols's *Never Mind The Bollocks* made Virgin one of the hippest labels in town.

As you walk on down Portobello, take a look at the **Portobello Court estate**. This 1950s development came about when the London County Council's slum clearance programme got the go-ahead to knock down the Victorian houses on this stretch and replace them with what you see today. Had those houses survived, they would now be prime real estate and worth a fortune.

As you continue to walk on you will notice

Portobello Road begins to flatten out and you will start to spot some of the myriad antiques arcades for which the area is famous. The oldest of these is **The Red Lion Arcade at numbers 165–9**, founded by local antiques dealer Susan Garth in 1951 and reportedly the first of its kind in London. There are around ten arcades in Portobello and Westbourne Grove, situated between Chepstow Villas and Elgin Crescent. They open on market days (generally Fridays and Saturdays) and offer a veritable Aladdin's cave of antiques and ephemera. Some arcades house as many as eighty stalls, selling everything from scientific instruments to Art Nouveau vases and vintage wristwatches. It is easy to lose track of time and spend an afternoon lost in these wonderful places.

Strolling on down Portobello you will begin to see some fruit and veg stalls, piled high with everything from potatoes and carrots to strawberries and bananas. You may also hear the booming voices of the stallholders, hollering out the price and provenance of their wares, 'Lovely punnets of English strawberries, only a paaaaaan.' Portobello market is built on fruit and veg. The trade was founded here over a hundred years ago.

There are still a handful of families who have had stalls here for several generations, trading long before the council licensed pitches, when the police would spend their days trundling up and down the street clearing away illegal traders. Look out for

Fruit and veg stalls remain at the heart of the market

Cheryl Collins stationed outside the Oxfam Bookshop at number **170 Portobello Road**. Cheryl is the third generation of her family to have traded on Portobello. She is one of the most well-connected people in the area – always saying hello to people passing her stall. Cheryl's day starts at 3.30 a.m. when she will go to a huge produce market near Heathrow, select and pick her goods, load up the van and head to her pitch on Portobello by 8.30 a.m. But the number of costermongers is dwindling fast. In the last ten years the street has lost at least three families who had held pitches here for over a hundred years – quietly admitting defeat in the face of supermarket dominance and the area's changing demographic.

Walking on, look out for the fruit and veg stall at the corner of **Talbot Road and Portobello**. If you are lucky you will see Peter Cain. There can't be many fruit and veg sellers who are former middleweight boxing champions, with 165 fights to their name. He also starred in Pier Paolo Pasolini's *The Canterbury Tales* in 1972. Peter's family are market stalwarts: his great-grandmother Dolly Cain started trading here after the First World War and was one of the first stallholders to be granted a fully licensed pitch in the late 1920s. During the Second World War, they worked on in spite of the Blitz, taking cover in the shelter in nearby Blenheim Crescent during the raids and opening up again as soon as the all-clear sounded. Buy some fruit to sustain yourself as we continue our walk.

In the early twentieth century, this junction at **Talbot Road/Blenheim Crescent** was the main venue for street entertainment and political demonstrations. A barrel-organ would provide the music, playing the tune of the day, and as the afternoon wore on things would often get quite lively as the crowd swelled in numbers and dancing and singing broke out. Another source of entertainment in the market can be found at the **Electric Cinema at 191 Portobello Road**, one of the oldest working cinemas in the country. The Electric opened for business on 27 February 1911. Designed by Gerald Seymour Valentin, it could seat up to 600. This was the era of the silent film, with only one projector, oil-powered lighting and bench seating, and most films lasting no longer than ten minutes. The cinema hit the headlines during the First World War

The Electric Cinema, one of the oldest working cinemas
in the country

when a group of locals stormed the building because
of a rumour circulating that the manager, of German
extraction, was signalling to Zeppelins from the roof.
In 1919, in an effort to keep pace with the times, the
Electric changed its name to the Imperial and operated a classic repertory program of three double bills
a week. But by the 1950s its popularity was dwindling,
as the new Odeon on Westbourne Grove provided
stiff competition with its comfortable seats and plush
interior. The Imperial became better known to locals
as the 'Bughole', offering cheap entry and all-night
shows. From 1969, a group of enterprising young hip-
pies led by John McWilliams, began hiring the cinema
on Saturday nights, showing alternative cinema under
the name *The Electric Cinema Club*. It proved such a
success that they soon took over full time. For a period,

they were the leading arts rep cinema in England, before others adopted their approach, from the Ritzy in Brixton to the Oxford Playhouse and Birmingham Arts Lab. They ran themed seasons showcasing genres such as film noir, gangster movies and musicals. The cinema is now part of the Soho House group and the bench seating and oil lamps have been replaced by a bar advertising champagne, where you can watch the film from the comfort of a sofa, an armchair or even a bed.

Continue down Portobello Road and pause outside **The Grain Shop at number 269 Portobello Road** which stands on the former site of **Ceres Grain Store** – one of the first health food shops in the country, and an integral part of the early health food movement. Ceres was founded by Craig and Greg Sams, two California-born brothers who helped kick-start the UK health food revolution. They had opened a restaurant called Seed in 1968, that became instantly popular and very fashionable – regular visitors included John Lennon, Marc Bolan and Pete Townsend. It soon transpired that their customers were keen to replicate the dishes that they were sampling at Seed in their own homes – and the idea for a health food shop stocking all the essentials of a macrobiotic diet was born. Ceres Grain Shop opened in March 1969, initially around the corner from here at 8A All Saints Road. It was the first natural food store in the country and soon spawned a bakery and a café. They also ran a travelling food kitchen, feeding the masses at the Isle of Wight Festival and the first Glastonbury Fayre in 1971. It wasn't long before other health food shops began to open up around the country – Infinity in Brighton, Suma in Leeds, Real Foods in Edinburgh and On the 8th Day in Manchester. It is wonderful to see The Grain Shop flourishing into the twenty-first century. It keeps the old hippy flame of the street alight – a welcome sight among the swish new boutiques, restaurants and nail bars. If you are hungry I heartily recommend a visit.

Continue to walk north on Portobello and you will come to the covered market under the Westway canopy. On Fridays and Saturdays this is taken over by **Vintage Clothes stalls**. Over the last twenty-five years Portobello market has become the go-to London destination for stylists, fashion designers, pop stars, fashion bloggers and fashion students. Fridays are the main day for the industry as designers from all the major fashion houses descend on the stalls, buying up pieces that they can use as 'inspiration'. The designs are then tweaked, stamped with the company name, and in the shops by the following season. Stroll around the stalls and marvel at the beautiful items on offer – from 1970s boutique labels like Bus Stop, Miss Mouse and Ossie Clark through to US military wear and rare denim brands. The birth of vintage fashion can be traced directly back to Portobello where it is still possible to find a unique bargain that you can be sure you won't find in any high street shop.

Once you tire of flicking through the rails of vintage clothes under the Westway, be sure to check out **The Acklam Village Market** on the other side of Portobello and also housed under the Westway. You will find stalls selling everything from cheeses and fresh bread to cupcakes and olives. Portobello has become something of a foodie heaven in recent years: you can sample Middle Eastern, African, German, Caribbean, Mexican, French and Spanish foods – all within a short walk of one another.

Head across Portobello and pause outside number **293**. In 1966 this was the site of I Was Lord Kitchener's Valet: one of the hippest fashion boutiques in Swinging London. Owners Ian Fisk and John Paul had graduated from a market stall, and specialised in selling Victorian military uniforms, along with assorted bric-a-brac. On Friday 27 May 1966, The Rolling Stones lead singer Mick Jagger stepped in, and after browsing the rails, slipped on a red grenadier guardsman's jacket, admiring himself in the mirror. He duly paid up and tucked his new purchase under his arm, walking out into the early summer's day. That evening he wore the jacket on *Top of the Pops*, when The Stones performed 'Paint It Black', and the following day there was a queue outside the shop, full of kids keen to emulate Mick's look. By the end of the day they had sold through all their stock. This marked the beginning of the military chic look that would prove a popular hit with other rock stars of the day, such as Eric Clapton of Cream and Jimi Hendrix. It is claimed that Pop artist Peter Blake got the idea for the *Sgt. Pepper* artwork while walking past this very shop a year later in 1967 and he sourced the Victoriana props for the sleeve from Portobello market. The military jacket has since passed into fashion history, echoing down the years with American designer Marc Jacobs adapting the look in 2002, leading to high street brands from GapKids to Primark launching their own versions.

Opposite at **278 Portobello** you will find **Honest Jon's Records**, one of the greatest independent record shops in the capital. Founded in 1974 they specialise in jazz, blues, reggae, dance, soul, folk and outernational sounds. One of their most loyal customers is local music legend Damon Albarn (lead singer of Blur and Gorillaz) who has described the shop as an educational place where he 'got his taste together'. In fact, he got on so well with the owners that they started the eponymous record label together, which has released a string of albums including a compilation series called *London is the Place For for Me*, excavating the music of young Black London, in the years after World War Two.

The last stretch of our walk continues taking us north on Portobello. Crossing over the junction at Radlington Road, you will begin to notice a more flea market feel to the stalls. Many tourists will turn around at this point, believing that this is the end of the market, but if you keep going you will get to Golborne

Road, which is well worth investigating. Alongside the delicious street food there is an eclectic range of vintage furniture shops and cafés. **George's Fish Bar at number 329 Portobello Road** is a neighbourhood favourite and you can't beat their fish and chips. What better way to finish our tour of the market?

WALK 2

– The Carnival –

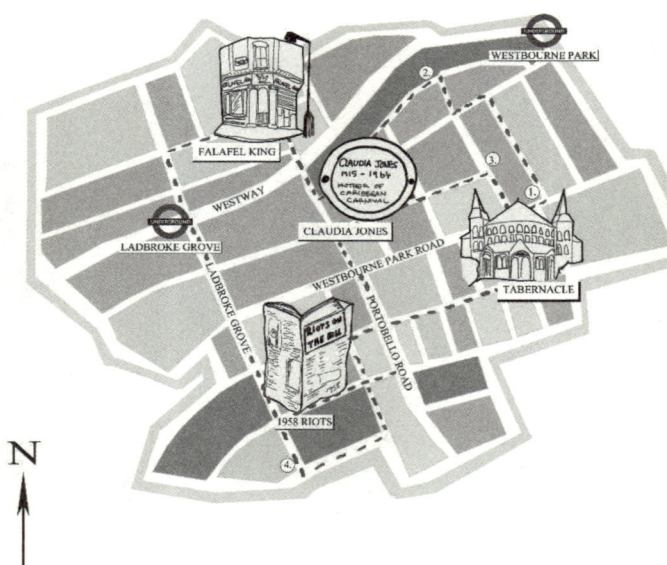

N

1. The London Free School, 26 Powis Terrace. **2**. Rhaune Laslett's Nursery, 34 Tavistock Crescent. **3**. The Mangrove Restaurant, 8 All Saints Road. **4**. 1976 Riots, corner of Elgin Crescent and Ladbroke Grove.

T he Notting Hill Carnival is the biggest annual street party in Western Europe, attracting upwards of 1.5 million people over the late August Bank Holiday weekend. Notting Hill's quiet, genteel streets are transformed into party central – with live music ranging from reggae to dub and salsa, thirty-seven static sound-systems, soca floats, steel bands and a parade down Ladbroke Grove. It is a celebration of the diversity of the neighbourhood and the city as a whole. This walk will introduce you to some of the carnival pioneers who helped shape the event into what it is today. The Carnival reflects the history of the neighbourhood from humble, sometimes troubled beginnings. It has risen to become an internationally recognisable event.

In 2016 Carnival celebrated its 50th anniversary, but its origins go deeper than that, dating back to a disturbing episode a few years before. Our first stop on this Carnival walk takes us to **9 Blenheim Crescent**. They say it's always the quiet ones you have to watch, and that is certainly so here. It would be easy to pass number 9 without so much as a second glance. It looks utterly inconspicuous amongst the smart boutiques and independent shops along this stretch of the street. But if you pause for a moment and let the tourists mill past you to the famous Travel Bookshop at number 13, your curiosity will be rewarded – for it was here on Monday, September 1st, 1958 that the worst race riots in post-war British history ignited when an estimated

300 black men clashed with a mob of white locals and Teddy Boys.

At the time number 9 housed Totobags café – the black community hang-out of the neighbourhood, where the recently arrived West Indian community (numbering around 7,000) would come to meet, drink, smoke, play dominoes and exchange news and gossip; soundtracked by the early sound system selectors King Dick, Baron Baker and Count Suckle. Certain daring bohemians like local author Colin MacInnes, musician Georgie Fame and even the occasional aristocrat like Winston Churchill's youngest daughter Sarah, would sometimes stop by for a night cap. But nobody had socialising in mind on that warm August evening as a confrontation became inevitable.

Relations between the West Indian community and the white community had been getting ever more strained for months, with divisions whipped up by a number of Fascist groups operating in the area. Principal among them were Oswald Mosley's Union Movement and The White Defence League, led by Colin Jordan, who had acquired a property at 74 Princedale Road, west of Ladbroke Grove near Holland Park. The tipping point for that weekend's violence had been an altercation on the Friday Night between a Jamaican man and his white Swedish wife, outside the nearby Latimer Road tube station. The couple had exited the station screaming and shouting at one another, embroiled in a bitter argument. A group of white locals tried to intervene and a scuffle broke out. No one could have foreseen the fallout from this seemingly unimportant event. News of the argument quickly spread as the white and black community took sides: the riots had been triggered, it was now just a matter of time before things turned ugly.

The black community had been turning the other cheek for months – just a week earlier a group of Teddy Boys had cruised the area 'Nigger Hunting' as they called it, leaving a trail of destruction in their wake – six people were left in hospital as the windows of homes and businesses owned by the black community were smashed and set alight. By Monday the 31st there had been a shift in feeling amongst the black community: enough was enough. They gathered at Totobags throughout the day, bringing with them an assortment of homemade weapons including meat cleavers, Molotov cocktails and knives. All afternoon, as more and more black men headed inside, a white mob gathered on the streets below. As their numbers grew, so did their confidence, and cries of 'Burn the Niggers out' were heard. Soon after 6 p.m. the upstairs windows flew open, a barrage of bricks and bottles were thrown onto the mob, the front doors were unbolted and the two factions began to fight one another in the street. Police sirens blared as six Black Marias arrived on the scene – Teddy Boys, white locals and black men, alongside eager reporters from the London media were caught in the violent melee. Mercifully no one was killed that night – the crowd dispersed and the reporters rushed back to Fleet Street to write about the events that would make sensational front-page news the next day.

If you continue to walk down Portobello Road to Tavistock Square, on the corner set up high on the wall you will see a Blue Plaque that reads: 'Claudia Jones, 1915–1964, Mother of the Caribbean Carnival in Britain organised an annual carnival from January 1959 as a community response to the 1958 August Bank Holiday Notting Hill riots.' Claudia had witnessed with horror the events of that weekend and felt that something must be done to help ease relations between the two communities. She was an extraordinary woman – Trinidadian born, she was raised in the United States but ultimately deported for her support of the Communist Party during the McCarthyite era. Landing in London she founded Britain's first major black newspaper *The West Indian Gazette.* After seeing the awful violence that weekend in Notting Hill (and reading of similar scenes in Nottingham where a riot also took place that weekend) she organised a meeting with community leaders, where the idea of a carnival to showcase the positive aspects of Caribbean culture was born. With that in mind, an indoor carnival event was held in January 1959, and for the following four years, attracting ever bigger crowds. Some two thousand attended the 1962 event at Seymour Hall in Marylebone, which included a beauty contest, calypso

Claudia Jones is commemorated with a plaque
in Tavistock Square

music and limbo dancing. Claudia's indoor carnival
events were cut short by her early death from TB and
heart disease on Christmas Eve of 1964 but she is now
quite rightly regarded as the mother of Caribbean carnival in Britain.

The next phase in the evolution of the carnival
takes us around the corner via St Luke's Road to **26
Powis Terrace**. Back in the spring of 1966, the London
Free School took over the basement of this formerly
dilapidated property, full of grand plans and high
ideals. The house was the London home of radical
writer John Michell, who liked the ideas that the Free
School espoused, and had donated his basement free
of charge to the group. It was far from perfect, being
damp, cold and filled with coal dust, but it was their
only option. The Free School has become something

of a footnote in the history of countercultural London – but it had the pedigree, being led by John 'Hoppy' Hopkins, one of the principal movers and shakers on the scene. A photographer, journalist and political activist, Hoppy had helped found the UFO Club. He had been inspired by the Free University movement he had witnessed on a trip to the United States the previous year and envisaged the London Free School as a combination of an adult education and a community education project. They talked of holding classes in everything from photography, art and literature to drugs and legal advice as well as creating a local newspaper. But despite regular meetings throughout the spring and summer of that year little of consequence materialised. One of the few concrete things to emerge from the time at Powis Terrace was their joining forces with Rhaune Laslett, a local community activist and organiser.

From Rhaune's home at 34 Tavistock Crescent (now demolished) she ran a nursery for local children that included an adventure playground in the back garden. Rhaune, a trained nurse of Native American and Russian lineage, had settled in the area in the late 1950s. She loved helping people and had a knack for bringing groups of like-minded people together. She became a well-known and liked member of the community, so much so that when boxer Muhammad Ali was in town for his May 1966 fight against Henry Cooper, he paid an unexpected visit to the Nursery, standing on the steps surrounded by adoring fans and sitting inside with the children, reading to them and having his photo taken. Rhaune joined forces with the London Free School and together they organised a street fair: the Notting Hill Fayre, held between Sunday 18th September and Sunday the 25th, 1966. It was a true community effort with everyone pitching in – a tipper truck was loaned from a local builder's merchants and decorated as a makeshift stage; a local fancy dress shop donated some costumes; and food and drink was pooled and shared amongst everyone attending. By all accounts it was a grand success, with a street procession kicking things off. In the evening, All Saints church hall was used for poetry readings, music, dance and those early Pink Floyd gigs (see pages 25 to 26). The event became an annual celebration which Rhaune and her husband Jim oversaw. They bowed out in 1970, handing the event over to the community to continue. Rhaune is commemorated by a Blue Plaque on Tavistock Square and Portobello Road.

It is important to remember that these carnival events of the late 1960s and early 1970s were still on a small scale: two steel bands and a 'jump up' street party around a neighbourhood of around three thousand people. There was a danger of things beginning to peter-out before our next Carnival pioneer emerged in 1973. Leslie Palmer, a young teacher from the area, was in charge of the carnival from 1973 to 1975, and was responsible for introducing the elements of carnival that we associate with the festival today – static sound-systems, masquerade bands, sponsorship and live radio broadcasts. If we stroll around to **All Saints Road**, a small street that houses one of the oldest record shops in the area, **People's Sound at number 11**, alongside **Portobello Music at number 13**, we can stop at number 8 where the **Mangrove Restaurant** stood until 1992. The Mangrove became the de-facto base for carnival activity year-round and by now numbers were reaching new heights of around 150,000 attendees. The Mangrove had been opened in 1968 by local resident Franck Crichlow who had previously run a café at 127 Westbourne Park Road called the El Rio. This had shot into the headlines during the Profumo affair in 1963, when it was revealed as one of the favoured meeting places of Stephen Ward and Christine Keeler. The Mangrove quickly established itself as a key meeting place for the black community along with white radicals and bohemians from the arts – Jimi Hendrix, Vanessa Redgrave, Bob Marley and Nina Simone all hung out here. A regular community newsletter called *The Hustler* was printed in the basement, with the restaurant always at the centre of things. If you are in the area during Carnival weekend, it is worth stopping by on the Saturday evening as the street is transformed into a rehearsal space for the Mangrove Steel band, who always sound superb and get everyone in the mood for the weekend to come.

The progress of the Carnival has not always been smooth, with several troubled years in the late 1970s and 1980s, when it seemed questionable whether Carnival would continue on the streets of Notting Hill. Let's head back down on to Portobello Road and walk south under the Westway and pause for a moment in the doorway of what is now **Falafel King at number 274 Portobello Road**. It was here in 1976 that some of the worst rioting and violence in the Carnival's history took place. Those attending that year reported seeing the police chasing a group of largely black carnival-goers from under the Westway towards where you are now standing. At some point the crowd realised they outnumbered the police and the tables were turned as they began to fight back. There followed widespread looting and fighting, shop windows were smashed, cars torched and property set alight. In the end over a hundred police officers and sixty members of the public were injured, some seriously. The police arrested sixty-six (mainly black) men with the subsequent trial seeing only seventeen charged resulting in only two convictions. It is generally agreed that the violence that erupted that day was due to heavy-handed police tactics. The previous, largely peaceful year, had seen around 300 police officers on duty – one year later that figure was ten times as many, with some 3,000 officers arriving in the neighbourhood, bussed in to 'keep the peace'. Against a backdrop of the Stop and Search laws and with race relations at an all-time low, it didn't take much to trigger violence – a pickpocket in the crowd was the excuse that the police used to begin to batter and advance on the carnival goers. Two young white men caught up in the riots that day were Joe Strummer and Paul Simonon of the Clash. If we walk across to **Ladbroke Grove a**nd stand on the corner of **Elgin Crescent** we will be close to where the young punks found themselves that day. Inspired by what they witnessed, they composed their incendiary debut single 'White Riot' in response. Released the following May and included on their debut album, it remains a classic statement of intent from the West London punk icons.

We finish our Carnival walk at the **Tabernacle, 34–5 Powis Square**. The building is set back from

The Tabernacle is at the heart of the Canival community

the square. Built in 1887, it has a beautiful curved Romanesque red brick façade with two small towers on either side of the entrance. Today the Tabernacle is a local arts and community centre and home to Carnival Village, one of the year-round bases of the event. In the run up to Carnival, you might be lucky enough to hear the Mangrove Steel Band rehearsing in one of the pan rooms at the back. If you have worked up a hunger after this Carnival walk this is a good place to sit down and have a rest. Keep an eye out for their permanent Carnival exhibition space next to the main bar – it has some iconic shots spanning the last fifty years – while the café menu offers a full English breakfast alongside Caribbean goat curry and plantain chips.

WALK 3

– Music, Literature and Film –

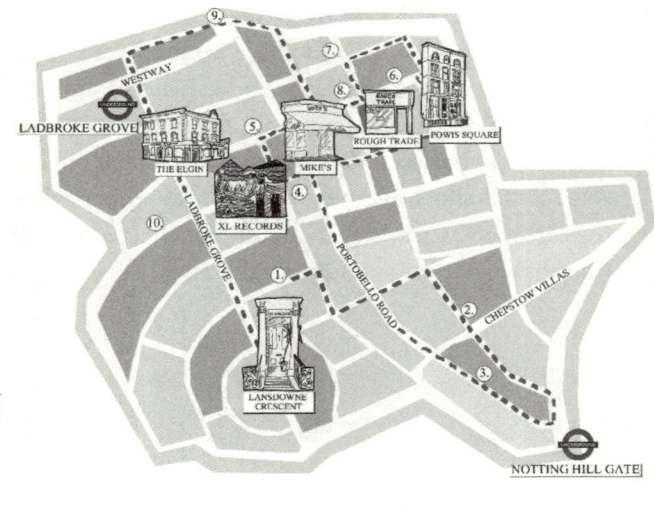

1. Joe Meek's home recording studio, 20 Arundel Gardens. **2**. Literary House, 24 Chepstow Villas. **3**. George Orwell's lodgings, 22 Portobello Road. **4**. The Travel Bookshop, 13 Blenheim Crescent. **5**. The Blue Door, 280 Westbourne Park Road. **6**. All Saints Church. **7**. Island Records Studios, 8–10 Basing Street. **8**. Scene in *A Hard Day's Night*, 20 All Saints Road. **9**. *Oz* & *Frendz* offices, 307 Portobello Road. **10**. Marc Bolan's flat, 57 Blenheim Crescent.

I read about Notting Hill long before I set foot in the neighbourhood, a well-thumbed paperback copy of Colin MacInnes's *Absolute Beginners* tucked into my duffel coat pocket at sixth-form college. Growing up in the rural wilderness of Herefordshire I dreamt about this bohemian enclave of London – I picked up mentions of Portobello Road market in Blur songs, tracked-down deleted Hawkwind and Quintessence albums and squinted through a poor-quality VHS copy of *Performance*, the seminal Nic Roeg and Donald Cammell film starring Mick Jagger. When I eventually moved to the capital it was the place I instantly headed for as I felt like I already knew it. This walk will introduce you to some of the places connected with film, music and literature in the neighbourhood – from recording studios to film locations and underground newspapers. Though it looks spruced up and affluent today, this area really was the countercultural capital of the city for a good portion of the 1960s and 1970s. Music of all genres flowed from these streets: from reggae; rock; punk; psychedelia; progressive-rock; folk and dub. They say if you listen hard enough, like one of London's lost rivers you can still hear these sounds bubbling away beneath the surface of the paving stones.

What better place to start than with the original rock'n'roll maverick, record producer Joe Meek, who had his very first home studio at **20 Arundel Gardens**? Meek is best known as the man behind 'Telstar' – the number 1 worldwide smash hit released in December 1962 and famously Margaret Thatcher's favourite record. Indeed, the honky-tonk piano used on that record was picked up on the Portobello Road market. Meek rented the ground floor flat in 1957, and had you visited at that time you could have been forgiven for thinking you had stumbled on the lair of a mad scientist in an English B-movie – reel-to-reel tape machines, echo units, microphones and amplifiers filled every inch of the tiny one-bedroom flat, with a labyrinth of cables dangerously criss-crossing the floor. Today it is not uncommon for a musician or producer to have a home-studio, but back in the 1950s it was unheard of. Meek was a trailblazer and this was the first of its kind in the neighbourhood. His tenure at Arundel Gardens was cut short when a record release party for his skiffle-produced tune 'Sizzling Hot' by Jimmy Miller and the Barbecues got a little out of hand with a reported 150 attendees. His long-suffering neighbours decided enough was enough and he received his marching orders soon afterwards.

Whilst rock'n'roll and skiffle dominated the airwaves of the late 1950s, the literary headlines were dominated by the so-called Angry Young Men – a loose-knit group of playwrights and novelists – and Notting Hill was home to some of its principal players. Walk on, up the slightly hilly incline to **24 Chepstow Villas**. Today it may look like just another beautiful Notting Hill house, with its pristine white paint gleaming in the sunshine – home to the city's most wealthy residents. But if we wind the clock back to the 1950s, we find a very different house and a very different set of inhabitants. This was a down-at-heel neighbourhood: many of the houses had fallen into ruin with the sash-window frames rotting, the white stucco crumbling, and the gardens an overgrown tangle. If you had visited this house in the 1950s or 1960s it would have likely been for a literary or arty gathering of some kind – for it was home to a revolving cast of writers, painters and actors. Back then the house was divided up into eight high-ceilinged rooms with fireplaces, along with a somewhat damp basement where Dylan Thomas was rumoured to have lived for a spell. During this time the postman would have delivered mail addressed to cult writer and troubled junkie Alexander Trocchi; Scottish painters Colquhoun and MacBryde; Welsh novelist and journalist Bill Hopkins; novelist Cressida Lindsay; painters John Eyles and Roland Jarvis; actor Dudley Sutton and, for a brief moment in 1956 the most famous of the whole lot, Colin Wilson, whose debut book *The Outsider* had made him an overnight sensation. When the follow-up *Religion and the Rebel* was published a year later and received a critical drubbing, he decamped to the solitude of Cornwall, handing on his room to local aspiring author Laura Del-Rivo, who still lives in the area, now in her eighth decade. She has published several novels since then, including her first, *The Furnished Room*, which was turned into

24 Chepstow Villas, formerly a hotbed of bohemian life and creativity

a film in 1963 and rechristened *West Eleven*. Starring Diana Dors and directed by Michael Winner, it is well worth tracking down as it was shot on location in and around Notting Hill and captures the seedy bohemian atmosphere in black and white.

Head back to Portobello Road and walk south to **number 22**, for it was here, in the winter of 1927, that a 24-year-old aspiring writer named Eric Blair, soon to become better known as George Orwell, lodged with a Mrs Craig after resigning his position as Chief Superintendent of The Indian Imperial Police in Burma. It was so cold he was forced to use a candle to warm his hands up before writing. Despite these trying conditions Eric wrote parts of *Down and Out in Paris and London* here and determined that he must become a writer. The rest, as they say, is history. We can safely assume that conditions inside number 22 have improved since then – the last time the property went on the market in 2014 it sold for £2.5 million.

Turn and walk on north down Portobello Road and you will begin to see the antique shops that dominate this part of the street. It was here that *Otley*, the 1968 Dick Clement directed film, was set and shot. A Swinging London spy caper, it failed to do well at the box office, but it is worth the price of admission for its opening sequence. It shows lead actor Tom Courtenay striding down this stretch of Portobello Road on a bright, sunny day. The street looks remarkably similar as Courtenay, playing the central character of Otley, a hapless, down-on-his-luck antiques dealer, waves a friendly greeting to the shopkeepers and stallholders. It would take a far more famous film, shot some thirty years later, that also uses Portobello market as its backdrop, to make the street internationally famous. *Notting Hill,* starring Hugh Grant and Julia Roberts, remains *the* calling card for the neighbourhood with fans coming from all over the world to track down the 'shop from the movie' and have their photo taken outside the fabled Blue Door. If you continue to walk down Portobello and turn left on to **Blenheim Crescent** you will find **The Notting Hill Bookshop at number 13** – this is the site of the former Travel Bookshop, the independent bookshop that director Richard Curtis used as the inspiration for the fictional Travel Book Company in the film. I worked at this shop for a number of years until rent and rates rises, along with online competition from Amazon made it untenable – thankfully it remains a bookshop and still has the same interior and shop fittings so you can step inside and have your own Hugh or Julia moment.

The Blue Door is one street further north at **280 Westbourne Park Road**. This front door is by far the most iconic and famous in the neighbourhood (perhaps even London) for it was here that William Thacker the bumbling bookseller played by Hugh Grant lived, and it is the location for the famous scene where Rhys Ifans, playing Thacker's housemate Spike, poses in his fetching grey Y-fronts for the world's media. The house was chosen as the location because it was, at the time of the film's production, Richard Curtis's home. The original Blue Door was sold off for charity, but the current residents have kept the door blue, so it makes for the ideal photo opportunity. Double back to **Mike's Café at number 12 Blenheim Crescent** for a coffee or a bite to eat before the next section of our walk. Mike's has been serving hearty fry-ups since 1962 and was featured on the cover of Traffic's 1971 album *Welcome to the Canteen*. Still a popular haunt for locals and tourists alike, Mike's holds out against the rising tide of gentrification. Here you are just as likely to see a market stall trader as a hedge fund manager.

Walk on, crossing Portobello Road, heading west from the junction with Blenheim Crescent, and you will find legendary independent record shop **Rough Trade Records at 130 Talbot Road**. Rough Trade was founded in 1976 and originally opened around the corner at 202 Kensington Park Road. It could not have timed its arrival at a more perfect cultural moment – 1976 was the year that punk broke and Rough Trade soon became a key outpost in the punk revolution. It acted as a community hub where gig posters could be Xeroxed, fanzines cut up and glued together, posters could be displayed and flyers could be handed out. Most importantly it offered a space for like-minded music freaks to meet and bond. Founded by a young corkscrew-curled Cambridge graduate named Geoff Travis, the shop soon evolved, spawning a distribution network and record label of the same name. Travis became more interested in the label side of things, and the staff bought the shop from him and moved

Rough Trade remains a cutting-edge independent record
shop over forty years since it first opened

around the corner to their current location in 1983.
Rough Trade the label went on to sign a raft of seminal
bands from The Smiths in the 1980s to the Libertines
and the Strokes in the new millennium. They remain
rooted in the neighbourhood with their offices located
a few streets away at 66 Golborne Road. The shop too
has flourished with branches in East London and New
York.

Leaving Rough Trade, we head further west down
Talbot Road to **All Saints Church**. Constructed in the
1850s in the Victorian Gothic Revival Style, it domi-
nates the square. Until the 1970s directly next to the
church stood a small hall of the most unassuming kind.
In its place today stands a rather dull-looking brick
building that is used as an old people's home, but it is
worth pausing for a moment because this site can lay

claim to being one of the most important in London's countercultural history. It was here on September 30th 1966, that Pink Floyd started a run of gigs that saw them transform from an R&B covers band (with the occasional original number) into fully fledged psychedelic pioneers. These gigs had been organised by their new managers Peter Jenner and Andrew King. Jenner and King were both the sons of vicars and knew that a church hall was a cheap and easy venue to hire – and this one was right in the middle of the most happening part of London. Perhaps it was not exactly the kind of venue the band had in mind when they signed up with them a month earlier but it paid off. By all accounts the hall housed a pretty basic set-up – at capacity it could fit 250 to 300 people, it had a high ceiling and polished wooden floor with a small raised platform at one end acting as the makeshift stage. But the surroundings didn't matter, the gigs were a success from the off, with queues around the block. It was during these gigs that they began to incorporate a light show into their act with the projection of wild colours onto the band as they performed, mixing with the music to mind-bending effect. One regular attendee was the so-called 'psychedelic schoolgirl' Emily Young. Young lived in nearby Kensington and was so entranced by the band that she came to as many gigs as she could. She would whirl around and dance, inspiring the Floyd's leader Syd Barrett to name their second single, released in the spring of 1967, 'See Emily Play'. The importance of these gigs was not just due to their place in the evolution of Pink Floyd but as stepping stones in the London countercultural scene. When the run of gigs ended in December a club night called the UFO was begun in a venue off Tottenham Court Road as a direct result of these gigs. It would become *the* hippest place to play and be seen over the next ten months, hosting Jimi Hendrix, The Soft Machine and of course Pink Floyd.

Keep walking westwards to Powis Square, surely one of the most storied of local rock'n'roll locations in the neighbourhood. Starting in the corner at number **25 Powis Square**, which was the home of Turner, the recluse rockstar in Donald Cammell and Nic Roeg's legendary film *Performance*. Though now regarded as a cult classic and a mainstay of film schools around the world, it was almost permanently shelved by Warner Brothers. The film merges London's ultra-violent gangster underworld with drug fuelled rock'n'roll, creating a psychological thriller that is at times deeply unsettling. Filmed during the turbulent summer of 1968 as students and workers took to the barricades in Paris and London, the atmosphere on set was no less dramatic. News of drug taking, mindgames and paranoia both on and off camera leaked out, as Mick Jagger cavorted with Keith Richards's girlfriend, Anita Pallenberg. A furious Keith reportedly sat outside in his Bentley, waiting to whisk her off set at the end of each day's filming. James Fox, who played the gangster hiding out at Chas's bohemian lair, became so immersed in the role that he had a nervous breakdown after the film was finished and did not make another movie for ten years. The finished cut was so violent and disturbing Warner Brothers did not know what to do with it. Eventually a heavily edited version was released in 1970. Although the interiors of the film were shot in an apartment in Knightsbridge (due to 25 Powis Square being too small to accommodate the cameras and lighting) the film is firmly rooted in the seedy, druggy Notting Hill of the time. In an uncanny footnote to the story, Mick Jagger's bandmate and founder of the Rolling Stones, Brian Jones, had lived at number **18 Powis Square** in July 1962 and was, by 1968, beginning to resemble the troubled character of Turner himself. It would not be long before he drowned in mysterious circumstances after taking a midnight swim in the pool of his Sussex home, on a hot July night in 1969.

Walk on to **8–10 Basing Street**, where until recently you would have found one of the most famous recording studios in London. **Island Records** bought the old church in 1969 and opened it as a recording studio in January 1970. The list of classic and huge-selling albums that were recorded here is eye watering, including The Eagles, Led Zeppelin, Jethro Tull, Bob Marley, Black Sabbath and Mott the Hoople. In 1975 the studio changed its name to Basing Street Studios until the early 1980s, when it was acquired by Trevor

Horn and ZTT Records and rechristened Sarm West. In 1984 the worldwide Band Aid supergroup smash 'Do They Know It's Christmas?' was recorded in studio 1, and a parade of stars stopped by to lay down their vocals. Sadly, like many studios of this era, the building itself was deemed to be worth more as luxury flats than as a recording facility and so it closed its doors in 2014.

Walk on to **All Saints Road**, which was the unlikely setting for a dose of Beatlemania in 1964 when the Fab Four stopped by to film a sequence for a *Hard Day's Night* featuring Ringo running away from a group of screaming girls, taking refuge in a junk shop at number 20. The shop has long since changed use but if you stop and listen very hard, some say you can still hear the screams of the fans as they chase the loveable mop-top.

Stroll on to **Portobello Road** and turn north towards the **Westway flyover** which you will see in all its concrete glory overhead. Stop underneath the flyover today and you will see shops and cafés, but back in the early 1970s when the road was only recently built, this no-man's-land was just being developed. During that time, it became a popular staging ground for gigs, and one of the most frequent and popular bands to play was Hawkwind. They would set up on a makeshift stage and play for free to the local community. If any band could lay claim to being the 'house band' of Ladbroke Grove and Notting Hill it would be them.

Continue on Portobello Road and walk north, looking out for **307 Portobello**, the former HQ of *Frendz* magazine, one of the key publications of the underground press of the 1970s. *Frendz* started life in December 1969. Originally entitled *Frendz of Rolling Stone*, it relaunched in 1970 simply as *Frendz*, and alongside *Oz Magazine* and the *International Times* was at the forefront of the alternative print revolution, both in terms of the subject matter it tackled and the graphic design it pioneered. *Frendz* featured the early work of photographer Pennie Smith, who went on to become one of the most respected rock photographers of the late twentieth century, taking iconic shots of everyone – Led Zeppelin, U2 and the Stone Roses, to name just a few. At *Frendz* she would often be paired with journalist Nick Kent, one of the most influential, and hard-living, rock critics of the 1970s.

Walk on to Ladbroke Grove and the **Elgin Pub at number 96**, another neighbourhood institution and important in the story of local legends The Clash, who drank and played here. It was at the Elgin in 1975, that Joe Strummer's pre-Clash band The 101ers were offered a weekly residency that led to a nine-month stay. The Clash formed when their nascent manager Bernie Rhodes introduced guitarist Mick Jones to singer Joe Strummer and bassist Paul Simonon in the spring of 1976. By the autumn they had a record deal with CBS. One of their most enduring singles 'White Riot' was inspired by the 1976 carnival riot (see page 24) As a band they wore their West London credentials resolutely on their sleeves, never forgetting where they came from. To mark the release of their landmark *London Calling* album in 1979 they played two free Christmas Day gigs under the Westway at Acklam Hall, now demolished, as a thank you to their loyal, local following.

Walk south down Ladbroke Grove and make a right on **to Blenheim Crescent**. Stop at number **57** and look up at the attic windows, for it was here in 1968 that Marc Bolan strummed an acoustic guitar composing 'Ride A White Swan' and bonding with original Tyrannosaurus Rex bongo player Steve 'Peregrine' Took. Wild haired and beautiful Bolan had matured from the pill-popping mod of his John's Children's days to become the epitome of The Hippie, quoting Shelley and Tolkien as he took another drag on that ever-present joint.

Staying on Blenheim Crescent, walk east towards Portobello Road, crossing Ladbroke Grove, and a few yards on, you will find the entrance to **Codrington Mews**. Like a secret street it peels off to the right. Mews like these are dotted all over the neighbourhood, dating from a time when horses required stabling, before the motorcar came along and changed everything. Set back from the road and often displaying their original stable doors, they are quiet pockets of calm amongst the hubbub of the city. If you walk down Codrington Mews you will come across a large black-and-white mural on the walls of 1 and 1a depicting the landmarks

Stanley Donwood's mural is a nod to the countercultural
heritage of the neighbourhood

of London being swept away by a tidal wave. It is *A
London Scene* by the artist Stanley Donwood, and was
commissioned by Richard Russell to cover the front
of the HQ of XL Recordings – the label he founded
in 1989. XL has been one of the few successful record
labels to emerge in the post-digital world, generating
huge sales with the likes of Adele, The White Stripes
and Radiohead.

For the last stop on this walk, we head back to
Ladbroke Grove and southwards to **22 Lansdowne
Crescent**, an address that has become a site of pilgrim-
age for those wishing to pay their respects to guitar
hero Jimi Hendrix who died here in the early hours of
Sept 18th 1970. At the time the building housed the
Samarkand Hotel where Jimi had checked in on the
17th, reportedly in good spirits, accompanied by his

on/off girlfriend Monika Dannemann. The pair had sat in the garden of the hotel drinking tea and laughing and, later, popped out to do some shopping in the hip Kensington Market just up the road. Jimi bought some shoes and a leather jacket, running into his old flame Kathy Etchingham – the last time they would meet. Reports differ as to the exact chain of events that unfolded that night, but it seems he ingested a large quantity of sleeping pills which he mixed with red wine, resulting in his choking on his own vomit some time in the early hours of the morning. At first it was thought he had committed suicide, since one of the first people on the scene, The Animals lead singer Eric Burdon, had found a note beside his bed with the words 'The story of life' scribbled on it. Since then, this has been attributed to a song lyric he was working on before he died. Interestingly this is not the only address in the neighbourhood that Hendrix is associated with – in 1967 he stayed at 167 Westbourne Grove, a house that was at the time painted Purple, reportedly inspiring his single 'Purple Haze'.

WALK 4

– Buildings, People and Places –

1. Tony Benn's home, 12 Holland Park Avenue. **2**. Avondale Park. **3**. Spanish Civil War mural. **4**. The Spanish School, 317–318 Portobello Road. **5**. Garcia and Sons, 248–250 Portobello Road. **6**. Café Lisboa, 57 Golborne Road.

T his walk will introduce you to some of the neighbourhood's most noteworthy buildings, the
people who lived in them, and the places that have
played a pivotal role in shaping this diverse community. Select some comfortable walking shoes, as we will
cover a lot of ground over the next few pages, both
geographically as well as through time.

We start at **Notting Hill Gate** and head west along
Holland Park Avenue. This is one of London's oldest thoroughfares, dating back to Roman times, when
it cut through an ancient forest full of wild boar and
deer. The road was a popular link between Oxford and
London, indeed it still is, with the London to Oxford
Bus service The Oxford Tube trundling along this road
today. The forest was gradually cleared in the Middle
Ages, and a village settlement appeared around what
is now Notting Hill Gate. Highway robbery was rife
here right up until the eighteenth century, when the
road was often in a state of disrepair, barely passable at
certain points. An Act of Parliament in 1714 allowed
for the collection of tolls to pay for the upkeep of the
road, and a turnpike, which was in operation until the
1860s, was erected around Notting Hill Gate.

Stop for a moment at **number 12 Holland Park
Avenue**. This was one of the first addresses that I
visited in the neighbourhood in the mid-1980s, for it
was here that Tony Benn, Labour MP, lived with his
wife Caroline, from 1952 until shortly before his death
in 2014. Benn was a relative of mine and when my

Veteran Labour MP Tony Benn's former home

family was in Town we would pop round for a cup of tea and a catch-up. Gathered in his comfortable sitting room, he would make us all a cup of tea and sit, pipe in hand, asking my sister and I how we were getting on at school and what we had planned for our time in London. His wife Caroline DeCamp Benn, who died in 2000, is commemorated with a Brown plaque on the front wall of the house, noting her contribution to education. She was co-founder of The Campaign for Comprehensive Education, which advocates for quality, all-ability schools open to all children, rather than selective schools with competitive exams. She was also co-founder, and a tireless supporter, of nearby Holland Park Comprehensive, where all the Benn children went.

Continue west on Holland Park Avenue and turn right onto Ladbroke Grove. Standing here at the southern end of Ladbroke Grove, on the brow of the hill, it is difficult to imagine that until the early eighteenth century this was agricultural land. Things began to change in 1819 when James Weller Ladbroke inherited the land from his grandfather and set the wheels in motion for a massive redevelopment that would see the area transformed over the next twenty-five years. In 1823, he tasked his most trusted architect Thomas Allason with the job of drawing up plans for a grand new building development to rival Mayfair and Belgravia. Allason came up with the idea of two large groups of houses backing on to communal gardens or a park, with a road running north to south through it (this would become Ladbroke Grove). Building work began soon afterward, but was interrupted by the so called 'Panic of 1825' financial crash. Builders downed tools and work ceased for the next seventeen years.

Walk on to the corner of **Ladbroke Square and Ladbroke Grove** and you will see one of the beautiful garden squares for which the area is so famous. Sadly, these squares are now the sole preserve of the wealthy residents who are lucky enough to live in the houses that back on to them. There are a total of sixteen in the neighbourhood. If you are looking for the garden featured in the film *Notting Hill*, where Hugh Grant and Julia Roberts spend a romantic evening, then head to **Rosmead Gardens** a few streets north of here – but it is best to just peek in through the railings rather than trying to climb in as they do in the film!

Walk on north down Ladbroke Grove and turn on to **Lansdowne Crescent**. This was once at the heart of a racecourse that briefly appeared here in the late 1830s. In 1837, with Weller Ladbroke's building work on hold, local entrepreneur James Whyte came up with the idea of creating a racecourse to rival Ascot and Epsom, later dubbed 'The Kensington Hippodrome'. He leased 140 acres of land and began to build a high wooden fence around the course. This did not go down at all well with some members of the community, not least those along **Pottery Lane** or 'Cut Throat Lane' as it was known at the time. This was a desperately poor slum area where few in the neighbourhood, save those unlucky souls who lived there, ever ventured. The fence cut across a public right of way and unsurprisingly it was continually broken down, with race meetings interrupted. In addition, the ground itself proved totally unsuitable for racing: the soft clay became easily waterlogged, with jockeys refusing to ride due to safety concerns. All in all, only thirteen meetings were held between 1837 and 1842, when Whyte finally admitted defeat and handed the lease back to Weller Ladbroke, and the building work was completed.

Let's go and see some of these former slums now. Walk west down **Lansdowne Rise,** along **Clarendon Road** and **Hippodrome Place** to **Walmer Road.** As you walk, look out for one of the many basement developments that have sprung up in the neighbourhood over recent years. The latest must-have accessory for the super rich, these so-called Mega Basement extensions incorporate swimming pools, cinemas, wine cellars, gyms and car parks built directly underneath the existing house. Kensington and Chelsea Council have seen applications for these so-called 'iceberg homes' rocket from thirteen in 2001 to over three hundred in 2016. The building process is extremely noisy and dirty – a high-powered drill bores its way through the ground below as a conveyor belt, set up in the front garden, rolls endlessly around, depositing its cargo of soil and rock into a waiting skip. Lorries come and go all day long. These developments take on average two years to complete. Unsurprisingly, there have been fierce battles between neighbours over such builds. Keep an eye out, as you are sure to see one as you walk through this part of the neighbourhood.

When you arrive in **Walmer Road** you are in the midst of what was once one of the poorest areas of

London, where the two principal occupations were pig-keeping and brick-making. Few non-locals ventured to this area, described in 1850, in the first issue of Charles Dickens's *Household Words* journal as '. . . a plague spot scarcely equalled for its insalubrity by any other in London'. On **Walmer Road** you can see the last remaining kiln that was used to fire bricks – the area was known for producing high-quality clay soil that was made into bricks in kilns like this one. The bricks were used by the burgeoning building industry all over the city and suburbs. The brick-makers lived next to the pig-keepers, who had been pushed west from Tottenham Court Road and Marble Arch as the city expanded. With no planning permission, slum conditions prevailed – there was no running water or proper sanitation, and pig and human excrement mixed in the large holes that had been dug for bricks. **Avondale Park**, located opposite the kiln, was the biggest of these holes and dubbed 'The Ocean' by locals. In 1892, it was filled in and turned into the green park it remains today. It is difficult to imagine the extreme levels of poverty that existed here. Today it looks so salubrious with expensive cars parked up outside the well-maintained houses that change hands for seven figure sums.

Walk north down Walmer Road and turn east to Clarendon Road, along Cornwall Crescent and then north along St Marks Road until you reach **22–29 St Andrew's Square**. You will have to take a leap of

The kiln on Walmer Road acts as a reminder of the brick-
making industry that flourished here in the 19th century

the imagination here, because the house and address you are looking for does not exist anymore. You are as close as it is possible to get to what was once 10 Rillington Place, perhaps the most infamous address in the neighbourhood. This was where John Reginald Christie lived between August 1943 and early 1953. Here he murdered eight women, burying them beneath the floorboards and in the small back garden. His actions were only uncovered after he had moved out of the property, three years after Timothy Evans, his former upstairs neighbour, had been wrongly accused, found guilty and hanged for murdering his wife and baby daughter, more likely the work of Christie. Christie had managed to pass himself off as an upstanding member of the community. He was even employed as a special constable during the war, and known for his pretended in-depth medical knowledge. He preyed on prostitutes, picking them up in local cafés and pubs. He would lure them back to Rillington Place where he would gas and strangle them. No one suspected him until after he had moved out of the property on 24 March 1953. The bodies of his last three victims were discovered by his upstairs neighbour Beresford Brown, behind the wall of a small alcove in the kitchen. A nationwide manhunt was launched and Christie was picked up by police officers on the embankment near Putney Bridge on 31 March. At the trial in June he confessed to the murders, entering a plea of insanity that was rejected by the jury, who found him guilty on all counts. He was hanged at Pentonville Prison a month later. As a grisly coda to this story, the 1971 film adaption of Ludovic Kennedy's bestselling book *10 Rillington Place*, starring Richard Attenborough, which charted the miscarriage of justice over the unsound conviction of Timothy Evans, was filmed on location in Rillington Place. As soon as filming wrapped up in October 1970, a team of demolition workers moved into the street and slowly tore down the houses with pick axes and shovels, making way for the Westway motorway.

Walk on along Lancaster Road and then north onto **Ladbroke Grove** and head underneath the **Westway flyover** followings its path eastwards, towards Portobello Road. Sitting on giant concrete stilts the road follows the railway line above to Paddington station and was originally conceived to combat congestion around Shepherd's Bush. Work began on it in 1964 and was completed in 1970. At the time of its completion it was the longest stretch of elevated motorway in Europe. Although it drastically cut travel time in and out of the city, its construction disrupted and displaced many in the community, a community that was already suffering from poverty and neglect. Despite a strong local campaign about the rehousing, it went ahead, and proved an immediate success in terms of traffic numbers with some 47,000 cars a day whizzing above Notting Hill just one month after it opened. The land directly underneath the motorway is operated by the Westway Trust and on Fridays and Saturdays market stalls pop up, making one forget there is a busy road directly above.

When you reach **Portobello Road** it is worth taking a moment to look at the colourful mural that adorns the wall under the railway bridge. It was unveiled in 2006 to commemorate the volunteers from Kensington who travelled to Spain to fight for the International Brigade during the Spanish Civil war of 1936–9. The neighbourhood has a strong and active Spanish community, with many Spanish immigrants settling here in the wake of the Civil War in the mid-1930s, fleeing General Franco's brutal repression. They were joined by a second wave in the 1970s, with a Spanish school founded a little further up **Portobello Road at 317–18**, hidden from view behind a brick wall, it is funded by the Spanish government and is at the heart of the Spanish community here. In addition, there is the excellent Spanish grocer **Garcia and Sons at 248–50 Portobello Road** which has been operating here since 1957, run by the same family from Malaga. Walk on north up Portobello Road.

We have now arrived at **Golborne Road**. Golborne has seen a lot of changes over the last decade, with the arrival of more upmarket boutiques and cafés, yet it still has a bohemian charm to it. Think of it as Portobello's daring younger sister. On Fridays and Saturdays, you will find the market in full swing here – with an emphasis on household furniture and homeware. This is where the bargains are to be found. It is worth noting the nondescript-looking building at **number 92**. Built in 1864, it was known as Peake House and until the 1980s was a chapel and ex-offenders' hostel. After a brief period in the 1990s when squatters took it over, it was bought by fashion designer Stella McCartney, and turned into her London HQ in 2003.

Walk on down Golborne and stop at the corner of **St Ervans Road**. Look up and you will see **Trellick Tower**, standing tall like a sentry guard keeping watch over the neighbourhood. Trellick was commissioned in 1966 by the Greater London Council and designed by revered modernist architect Erno Goldfinger, with work completed in 1972. It stands 98 metres tall and echoes Goldfinger's design for the slightly smaller Balfron Tower in Poplar, East London. With its distinctive service tower standing next to the main structure, and linked by a walkway on every third floor, it divides opinion – some see it as a beautiful example of Modernist design, others think it ugly and grey. Writer Ian Fleming, creator of James Bond, so loathed Modernism, and Goldfinger's version of it in particular, he named an arch villain after him. Goldfinger had envisaged a concierge for the building, and even a vetting process to decide on tenants, but these suggestions were ignored by the Council. By the time of its completion, the grand idea that structures like this would herald new 'streets in the sky' was no longer as fashionable, as the social problems

Trellick Tower keeps an eye on the neighbourhood from its position at the end of Golborne Road

associated with them became clear. In the 1970s, and much of the 1980s, Trellick had a reputation for drugs and violence. Eventually, a concierge and intercom system was added in the mid-1980s, and of the 217 flats that make up the building, a significant proportion are now privately owned, and highly desirable addresses at that. Trellick Tower has appeared in numerous songs, books and films over the years, including as an inspiration for J. G. Ballard's dystopian novel *High Rise*, in Martin Amis's iconic *London Fields* novel and in the Blur song *Best Days*. We have reached the end of our walk, and what better way to finish than with one of **Café Lisboa**'s delicious Pasteis de Nata. This Portuguese institution at **57 Golborne Road** provides the ideal place to rest your weary feet and mull over all that you have seen.

– Postscript –

During the writing of this book the neighbourhood suffered a catastrophic event – on 14 June 2017, a fire broke out at the twenty-four-storey Grenfell Tower block on Grenfell Road, causing seventy-one deaths and over seventy injuries. The local response was immediate: the community rallied round, donating money, food, shelter and clothing. Questions over how such a tragedy happened remain unanswered, with the local and national government's response seen as slow and inadequate. An ongoing inquiry into events leading up to the fire is under way. I would remind anyone who walks past the site of Grenfell to be respectful. This is a place of mourning – it is not encouraged to take photos. There are plans to turn the site into a permanent memorial for those who lost their lives here.

– Directory –

The Abbey Court
20 Pembridge Gardens W2 4DU
0207 221 7518
www.abbeycourthotel.co.uk
Quiet townhouse hotel with pretty antique furniture, great value family rooms for four, with four-poster bed and breakfast included. From £219 per night. Singles with bathrooms from £108 per night.

Bowden Court
24 Ladbroke Road W11 3NN
0203 740 2429
www.lhalondon.com/bowden-court/
A LHA hostel in a 1930s mansion block in the heart of Notting Hill. There's a gym, common room and study on site, breakfast is included, no en-suite rooms, but a shared four-bed dorm room and singles are very reasonably priced. From £21 per person per night.

The Laslett Hotel
8 Pembridge Gardens W2 4DU
0207 792 6688
www.living-rooms.co.uk/hotel/the-laslett
Named after Rhuane Laslett, Notting Hill Carnival pioneer,

The Laslett is arty, stylish and quirky, and it is attracting a lot of positive reviews. Rooms from £190 to £400 a night.

The Leinster Hostel
44–46 Leinster Gardens W2 3AT
0203 740 9845
www.lhalondon.com/leinster-house
In a classic Notting Hill stucco house this hostel is run by LHA, a charity which endeavours to provide affordable accommodation in London. Simple, clean, sociable and cheap. Shared single-sex dorm rooms from £24 per person per night, single rooms from £36 a night.

The Portobello Hotel
22 Stanley Gardens W11 2NG
0207 727 2777
www.portobellohotel.com
Beautiful town house hotel, where rock meets chic. Blur's Damon Albarn was once a barman here. Writer Jean Rhys would drink on Van Morrison's tab. Kate Moss and Johnny Depp filled the Victorian bath in room 16 with champagne and Alice Cooper mislaid one of his pet snakes here (pets are welcome). From £190 to £350 a night.

Portobello House
225 Ladbroke Grove W10 6HQ
0203 181 0920
www.portobellohouse.com
Lively, affordable and fun, this converted pub offers pretty rooms, lots of live music and events. Rooms from £110 to £210 including breakfast.

ENTERTAINMENT, CULTURE, AND THE ARTS

Acklam Village Market

4–8 Acklam Road W10 5TY

www.acklamvillage.com

Under the Westway, Acklam Village continues the tradition of live music in Notting Hill. Also a street food market, DJs, visual and performance art, cabaret, yoga and mini festivals.

The Electric Cinema

191 Portobello Road, Notting Hill

London W11 2ED

0207 908 9696

www.electriccinema.co.uk/portobello

Choose from armchairs a sofa or a double bed, and settle down with snacks and drinks under a cashmere blanket for a unique cinematic experience. The Electric Diner, next door, is open until midnight for post film munchies.

The Gate Theatre Notting Hill

11 Pembridge Road W11 3HQ

0207 229 0706 (box office)

www.gatetheatre.co.uk

Above the Prince Albert Pub, The Gate Theatre opened in 1979 founded by Lou Stein. The tiny 75-seater theatre has been hugely influential, and is much loved by London thespians from Jude Law to Kathy Burke.

Notting Hill Arts Club

21 Notting Hill Gate W113JQ

0207 460 4459

www.nottinghillartsclub.com

Great mix of art and photography gallery and club with live acts and DJs. A sensibly priced drinks list and an inclusive atmosphere, local luminaries like Mark Ronson pop in, but the real stars are on the dance floor.

The Print Room at the Coronet
The Coronet, 103 Notting Hill Gate W11 3LB
0203 642 6606 (box office)
www.the-print-room.org
Built as an opera house in 1898, the Coronet has been a theatre, a cinema, and is now a theatre again.

Tabernacle
35 Powis Square, off Portobello Road W11 2AY
www.tabernaclew11.com
Live music, theatre, cinema, exhibitions, classes and courses take place here. Plenty of space to sit inside and out, serving a full English breakfast, West Indian curried goat, Indian Rotis and Dahls with a great value drinks menu.

BOOKSHOPS

Books for Cooks
4 Blenheim Crescent W11 1NN
0207 221 1992
www.booksforcooks.com
A neighbourhood institution. Arrive early to avoid disappointment – no pre-booking – and enjoy a three-course set menu with recipes taken from one of their vast library of books: vegetarian on Tuesdays, fish on Fridays. If you love it you can buy the book and cook it at home.

Book & Comic Exchange

30 & 32 Pembridge Road W11 3HN

0207 598 2233

This brilliant bookshop stocks fiction, non-fiction, biography and is strong on music and culture, with a vast array of comics. You can trade in your unwanted books and magazines, just make sure you take along ID and something with your printed name and address on.

Daunt Books Holland Park

112–14 Holland Park Avenue W11 4UA

0207 727 7022

www.dauntbooks.co.uk/holland-park/

The West London outpost of the famous bookseller-led Daunt chain. Pop in and browse the skilfully laid out selections on the front tables or ask for a recommendation from the well-read staff. Remember Daunt lay out their stock by country rather than A–Z by author which can lead to some interesting discoveries.

Lutyens & Rubinstein Bookshop

21 Kensington Park Road W11 2EU

0207 229 1010

www.lutyensrubinstein/bookshop/

Since opening in 2009 Lutyens and Rubinstein has become well known as a book lovers' destination of choice – the shop itself is beautifully designed with an unparalleled selection, the emphasis is on excellence in writing and narrative across a broad range of genres from fiction to children's books. They run an extensive events programme, see their website or pop in store for details.

The Notting Hill Bookshop
13 Blenheim Crescent W11 2EE
0207 229 5260
www.thenottinghillbookshop.co.uk
On the site of the former Travel Bookshop (the inspiration for The Travel Book Company in the *Notting Hill* film) the Notting Hill bookshop carries on that tradition. They offer a range of genres from fiction to non-fiction and biography.

LIFESTYLE SHOPS

281 Portobello Road
281 Portobello Road W10 5TZ
0208 960 2277
www.281portobelloroad.com
A collective of independent fashion & designer boutiques, lovely Forties-style naughty knickers at What Katie Did, unique, fun and practical children's clothes from Sasti, contemporary jewellery with an ethereal beauty handmade on site at ISIS, and modern pieces inspired by organic forms from Sarah Bunting and animal print T-shirts from Menagerie all washed down with a coffee from the Petit Café.

Aesop
61 Golborne Road W10 5NR
0208 964 9731
westbourne@aesop.com
Aesop shops are a sensory delight: they smell delicious and each store is architect-designed, respecting the location and history of the area. There is a smaller Aesop store at 227 Westbourne Grove, designed by Ilse Crawford.

Agent Provocateur

303 Westbourne Grove W11 2QA

0207 243 1292

www.agentprovocateur.com

Co-founded by Joe Corré, the son of Punk instigators Vivienne Westwood and Malcolm McLaren. Agent Provocateur sells Hollywood-pin-up circa-1940-inspired underwear. While Joe has moved on, this lingerie shop remains a London style experience not to be missed.

Alice's Antiques

86 Portobello Rd W11 2QD

0207 229 8187

Opened in 1887, Alice's stands out even among the colourful antique shops of the Portobello Road. It's also where Paddington Bear visits his antique dealer friend Mr Gruber for tea and wisdom, now selling a mix of antiques, reproductions and giftware.

Ally Capellino

312 Portobello Road W10 5RU

0208 964 1022

www.allycapellino.co.uk

portobello@allycapellino.co.uk

Designer Alison Lloyd has been at the forefront of London fashion since 1980. Her timeless, durable anti-fashion bags and accessories are pared-back classics.

The Antique Clothing Shop

282 Portobello Road W10 5TE

0208 964 4830

www.282portobello.london

Specialising in unisex Barbours, riding jackets, tweed, fleeces, hats and boots, this store has a distinctly Horse & Country air.

Army Classics

49 Pembridge Road W11 3HG

0207 221 7117

The basement of this friendly and established surplus store is the place to pick up army jackets from around the world. The owners recommend checking out the French Army uniform, although brightly coloured dress uniform jackets as worn by a young Mick Jagger are also available.

Barham Antiques

83 Portobello Road 83 Portobello Road W11 2QB

0207 727 3845

www.barhamantiques.co.uk

Barham Antiques has one of the largest stocks of antique boxes, tea caddies, champagne & whiskey glasses, and accessories anywhere in the UK. Their hugely knowledgeable and friendly staff are welcoming to all visitors.

Couverture & The Garbstore

188 Kensington Park Road W11 2ES

0207 229 2178

www.couvertureandthegarbstore.com

This concept store stocks an eclectic mix of clothing, accessories and homeware. The townhouse store focuses on independent labels with 'a story to tell'.

Graham & Green
4 Elgin Crescent W11 2HX
0207 243 8908
www.grahamandgreen.co.uk
Beautifully presented mix of jewellery, gift wrap and cards, furniture, and accessories from across the globe.

Honest Jon's
278 Portobello Road W10 5TE
0208 969 9822
www.honestjons.com
Honest Jon's has operated in Notting Hill since 1974. Specialising in Blues, Soul, Reggae, Jazz, Soul Funk and much more besides. The racks overflow with vinyl and the staff are knowledgeable and friendly.

Kleanthous Antiques
144 Portobello Road W11 2DZ
0207 727 3649
www.kleanthous.com
Since 1969 the Kleanthous family have dealt in antique watches. These are the gentlemen to ask which watch Sean Connery wore as James Bond, and their shop is the place to buy it.

Lyndons Art and Graphics
Unit 1, 216 Kensington Park Rd W11 1NR
0207 727 5192
Cards, stationery and art supplies, for the arty Notting Hill set.

Oxfam Shop
144 Notting Hill Gate W11 3QG
0207 792 0037
Well stocked with fiction, non-fiction, biography and much more. Worth popping in to pick up a bargain or two, they also have a decent vinyl and CD selection if you prefer physical formats to streaming!

Paul Smith
Westbourne House 122 Kensington Park Road W11 2EP
0207 727 3553
www.paulsmith.com
A beautiful double-fronted stucco townhouse, very subtly transformed, makes this Paul Smith's favourite among his shops.

Pedlars General Store and Café
128 Talbot Road, Notting Hill W11 1JA
0207 727 7799
www.pedlars.co.uk
Pedlars offer a curated, considered and beautifully designed range of homewares, stationery and gifts. Their café menu includes a variety of top-notch sandwiches and cakes made fresh every day, as well as homemade cold and hot drinks, amazing Allpress coffee and good music, fast Wi-Fi and comfy chairs.

Rellik
8 Golborne Rd W10 5NW
0208 962 0089
www.relliklondon.co.uk

The fashion editor's choice vintage clothes shop: serious couture and ready-to-wear history from Ossie Clark to Vivienne Westwood.

Rough Trade

Rough Trade West 130 Talbot Road W11 1JA
0207 229 8541
www.roughtrade.com
Rough Trade was founded around the corner on Kensington Park Road in 1976 before moving to this location in 1983. They stock a huge range of vinyl and CDs alongside books and fanzines. If you need a recommendation then the staff are always first on new artists and bands.

Sheila Cook Textiles

26 Addison Place W11 4RJ
0207 603 3003; 07798 700 294
www.sheilacook.co.uk
By appointment only, so phone first to shop a unique collection of fabrics, clothes and 'extravagances'. Mary Poppins-style Victorian suits, *Great Gatsby* dresses, and 1980s bling jewellery.

The Spice Shop

1 Blenheim Crescent W11 2EE
0207 221 4448
www.thespiceshop.co.uk
Unique little shop, selling 2,500 types of spice in brilliant yellow tins. The owner, Birgit, also teaches at Books for Cooks across the road.

Sub Couture

204 Kensington Park Road W11 1NR

Tel: 0207 229 5434

www.subcouture.co.uk

Sub Couture started out as a small fashion label during the early 1990s with this shop opening in 1995. Initially they only stocked the Sub Couture label but later began to include complementary designers and accessories. Their ethos is to introduce and nurture new designers alongside existing labels such as Patrizia Pepe, Hale Bob, Dr Denim and Vivienne Westwood's Melissa Shoes.

Supra

249 Portobello Road W11 1LT

0207 243 3130

www.supralondon.com

Men and women's fashion store selling edgier labels, big on modern Nordic and Continental brands.

Wasoukan by Noriyuki Ikeda

293 Westbourne Grove W11 2QA

0203 637 5010

www.wasoukan.eu

This beautiful little store is London's first matcha café and kimono boutique launched by Tea Master Noriyuki Ikeda. Here you can book a tea ceremony, learn how to wear a kimono and, once you have mastered that, go on a curated outing wearing it with other like-minded people.

Wild at Heart
222 Westbourne Grove W11 2RH
0207 727 3095
www.wildatheart.com
Wild at Heart is one of the most celebrated British florists, renowned for luxurious hand-tied bouquets and high-profile weddings.

EATING AND DRINKING

Beach Blanket Babylon
45 Ledbury Road W11 2AA
0207 229 2907
www.beachblanket.co.uk
This long-established restaurant and bar is set in a Georgian town house, candle lit, and decorated in opulent rococo style. There's a ballroom, chapel and even a scullery for the full upstairs-downstairs experience.

Café Lisboa
57 Golborne Road W10 5NR
0208 968 5242
www.cafelisboa.co.uk
Famous for their Portuguese patisseries of every kind, oozing with custard, or chocolate, or cream, including the famous Pasteis de Nata and Bolo de Arroz, and the annual appearance of the Bolo Rei Epiphany cake, in the form of a Magi's crown, with crystalised fruit for jewels.

Clarke's Restaurant

124 Kensington Church Street W8 4BH

0207 221 9225

www.sallyclarke.com

Sally Clarke has been serving simple, seasonal food, from a constantly changing, set-price menu for over thirty years. A delicatessen and shop has been added to her small, but influential empire. Lucian Freud used to breakfast there most mornings, and painted Sally's portrait.

The Coffee Plant

180 Portobello Road W11 2EB

0207 221 8137

www.coffee.uk.com

Owner Ian Hensall started out roasting coffee beans on Portobello Market in 1987 and has been part of the community ever since. The store roasts its own beans and sells a vast array of coffees with organic and fairtrade a speciality. This is a coffee shop with a heart – politically and socially engaged too.

Cottons

157–9 Notting Hill Gate W11 3LF

0207 243 0090

www.cottons-restaurant.co.uk

With a Guinness World Record winning 372 varieties of rhum, Cottons has been serving up the Carribean vibe since the 1980s, aided by live reggae and jazz.

The Cow

89 Westbourne Park W2 5QH

0207 221 5400 or 0207 221 0021

www.thecowlondon.co.uk

The Conran family changed the way London looks, dresses, shops and eats. The Cow is one of Tom Conran's contributions – a chic dining room, and simple saloon bar kitchen. It's very easy to enjoy.

Da Maria 'A corner of Naples in London'
87b Notting Hill Gate W11 3JZ
Tel 07733 143191 & 0207 792 4491
www.damaria.co.uk
Squeezed next to The Gate Cinema, Da Maria's is a tiny, inexpensive and much loved local opened by the Ruoccos in 1980. Great Neopolitan food and wine served by owners who place family, SSC Napoli, and conviviality before cash.

The Distillery
186 Portobello Road W11 1LA
0203 034 2233
www.the-distillery.london
Gin's the thing and The Distillery offers four floors of it, distilling Portobello Road gin on site. Food is British retro: Scotch eggs, hand-cut chips, pork pies. If it all gets too much, you can get a room there.

The Elgin
96 Ladbroke Grove W11 1PY
0207 229 5663
www.theelginnottinghill.co.uk
A long-standing neighbourhood favourite that boasts an original listed bar, bustling outside area, real wood fireplaces and British seasonal menu. This is where Joe Strummer's pre-Clash band the 101ers held a residency in 1975, securing a place in rock'n'roll history.

Geales

2 Farmer St W8 7SN

0207 727 7528

www.geales.com

This once humble fish-and-chip restaurant has morphed into a stylish restaurant and wine bar. Outside tables on Farmer St are perfect for al fresco eating on summer evenings.

George's Portobello Fish Bar

329 Portobello Road W10 5SA

0208 969 7895

Rated as among the top fish-and-chip shops by Michelin-starred chef Alain Ducasse, George's is a much-loved local institution.

The Grain Shop

269A Portobello Rd W11 1LR

0207 229 5571

Vegetarian and vegan food shop selling a range of hot and cold dishes alongside salads, cakes and breads. Priced by size of tray, selling healthy and tasty food for the masses.

Kensington Place

201 Kensington Church St W8 7LX

0207 727 3184

www.kensingtonplace-restaurant.co.uk

A favourite of Princess Diana's, Kensington Place opened in 1987 and has been going strong ever since. It retains a breezy, approachable charm, with a menu big on fish. They also have a fish shop next door.

The Ledbury
127 Ledbury Road W11 2AQ
0207 792 9090
www.theledbury.com
With two Michelin stars, and voted one of the 100 best restaurants in the world, Brett Graham is clearly a very talented chef. This is serious fine dining, but with a welcoming Aussie vibe.

The Malabar
27 Uxbridge Street W8 7TQ
Tel 0207 727 8800
www.malabar-restaurant.co.uk
One of the best Indian restaurants in London for quality and value, with a beautifully uncluttered dining room that belies its thirty-plus years of serving. Has great charm, and a short and keenly priced menu. The Malabar also offers a leisurely buffet lunch to enjoy with the Sunday papers.

Mediterraneo
37 Kensington Park Road W11 2EU
0207 792 3131
www.mediterraneo-restaurant.co.uk
The local upmarket Italian restaurant since 1998. No pizza. Sister restaurant is Osteria Basilico at 29 Kensington Park Road.

Mike's Café
12 Blenheim Cresc W11 1NN
0207 229 3757
A Notting Hill institution opened in 1961, the original wooden benches have since been replaced with Union Jack

upholstered thrones. Mike's Café offers a generous full English breakfast, and is one of the few places left in London serving worker's classic liver & bacon.

Mr Christian's Limited
43 Portland Rd W11 4LJ
0207 229 0501
www.mrchristians.co.uk
Old-school deli making British classics such as shepherd's pie and sausage rolls, alongside sandwiches and breads.

Pizza East
310 Portobello Road W10 5TA
0208 969 4500
www.pizzaeast.com
From the Soho House group, Pizza East is two floors of easy-going buzz, with a roof terrace.

Rum Kitchen
6–8 All Saints Road W11 1HH
0203 668 2538
www.therumkitchen.com
Caribbean food washed down with rum-based cocktails, a taste of carnival all year round.

Trailer Happiness
177 Portobello Road W11 2DY
trailerh.com
Tiki cocktail lounge specialising in rum based drinks since 2003, with live DJs at the weekend, as kitsch and classic as Vladimir Tretchikoff's 1950s paintings.

Uxbridge Arms
13 Uxbridge Street W8 7TQ
Tel 0207 792 1362
www.theuxbridgearmskensington.co.uk
Opened in 1869, this cosy independent pub is a great place
to watch the winter weather from the window seat, nursing a
mulled wine or a craft ale.

– Acknowledgements –

Thanks to Kim Kremer at Notting Hill Editions for commissioning the book and being so supportive; my agent Jane Turnbull, a West London resident herself, for her input and ideas; Travis Elborough who connected me with Notting Hill Editions in the first place; Bob Stanley for the much needed coffee breaks; Tom Vague for his vast West Eleven knowledge; my partner Gudrun and son Rowan who have endured endless walks around Notting Hill in all weathers; my parents John and Annie who introduced me to Notting Hill over thirty years ago; and Joe Perman Turnbull for his stylish maps and photos.

ノッティングヒル
ウォーキングガイド

–

ジュリアン・マッシュ

トモコ・オルダーソン訳

日本語版は、本書の内容を海外の読者によりわかりやすくするために、原文に加筆修正をしています。

Contents

キム・クレマー

– 出版に寄せて –

ノッティングヒル・エディションズは、私の父ト
ムクレマーが2011年に創設した出版社です。
彼は1963年、セブン・タウンズという玩具会社をケ
ンジントンパーク通りに設立し、ノッティングヒルで
の企業家人生を始めました。その会社は彼自身の
発明した玩具を販売すると同時に、優れた玩具発
明者の商品の販売特許を取得していました。ルービ
ック・キューブはそんな彼の先見の明を象徴する大
きな成功でした。(こんなパズルは売れないと散々
いわれていたのですから…)。セブン・タウンズは今
もウエストボーン・グローブの工房で玩具を作り続
けています。

トムはトランスバニアで生まれ1950年代に英国に
移民として移り住み、そしてエジンバラ大学で私の
母、レディ・アリスン・バルフォーと出会いました。身
分の違いすぎる2人でしたが、なぜか即座に惹かれ
合いました。アリスンは皆によくこう言っていたもの
です。「この奇妙で身なりにかまわないハンガリア人
は、私の人生に深くかかわる大切な人物になると瞬
間的に感じたのよ」と。彼らは周囲の反対を押し切っ
て一緒に暮らし始めました。結婚もせず、金銭的な援
助もないまま、結局このノッティングヒルにたどり着
き、50年代の、自由で開かれたこの土地に終の棲家
を見つけたのです。セントジェームス・ガーデンの水

道のない古い家を買い、プロのギャンブラーに空いた部屋を貸していましたが、賃貸料が支払われるのは賭けに勝ったときだけでした。そんなだだっ広い天井の高い家で、兄、姉、私は育ちました。アイルランド人洗濯屋とイタリア人レストランオーナーの隣人たち、「ラグ・ボーン！」と叫びながら、廃品回収者が馬でトラックを引いて、近所のくず集めをしていた光景を思い出します。

　アリソンはジャーナリストやフードライターとして働き、トムは職を転々としながら、一瞬のひらめきでセブン・タウンズを創設しました。ノッティングヒルには昔も今も、豊かな文化と独特の雰囲気、そして新しい先駆者を生み出す肥沃な土壌があると思います。エキセントリックなトランスバニア出身のユダヤ人トムもまた、ノッティングヒルを真の故郷だと感じ、一生涯心底この土地に魅了され続けた住人の一人でした。

　玩具メーカーとしての事業の成功のあと、トムは80歳になって、残りの人生を文学への熱い思いに捧げようと考えました。めまぐるしいデジタル文化の時代、人々の時間はどんどん短くなり、本は容赦なく切り捨てられています。そんな中で、彼は随筆の技法を復活させ、いつまでも楽しめる美しい装丁の本を出版することを決意したのです。象徴的な名前は誰の耳にも残ると考え、新しい事業は『ノッティングヒル・エディションズ』と命名され、ノッティングヒル・ゲートのニューカム・ハウスでその産声をあげました。

　父の希望で、私は2014年にその出版社の一員になり、それから彼が他界する2017年まで一緒に仕事を

しました。もし彼が今生きていてこの本を手に取ることができたら、きっとこう言うでしょう。—「ごもっとも！世界中のどこを探してもノッティングヒルみたいな場所はありゃしないよ。」と

　ジュリアン・マッシュの本は、この注目すべきロンドンの一角、ノッティングヒルの文化、建築、社会の歴史的散策です。心地よいソファーに座って、想像力を駆使しながら歩いてもよいし、シューズを履いて、歩道を闊歩しながら革命的な住人達の足跡をたどるのもいいでしょう。

ノッティングヒルにようこそ、そして、楽しいウォーキングになりますように！

ジュリアン・マッシュ

− はじめに −

ウォーキングは、間違いなくその街を探検し土地勘を得る最良の方法だ。柵に囲まれた入口もなければチケットを買う必要もない。快適な靴を選んでコースをきめたら、ひょいと出かけるだけ。そんな風に考えて、僕は知らない街に来た時はできるだけ歩いてみることにしている。たまに行先を決めずに気の向くまま歩いてみることもある。AからBの移動だけだったら知りえなかった、意外な発見をすることがあるから面白い。

　僕はロンドンに来て10年あまりこのノッティングヒルに住んでいる。そしてウィーキングは、ノッティングヒル（その風景だけでなくそこに住む人たち）の秘密を紐解く重要なカギだった。ポートベロ・マッケットを歩いて、露店の人たちとおしゃべりし、行きつけの喫茶店で顔なじみに会うなかで、僕は一生涯の友と仲間を見つけたのだ。

　都会に住んでいると、同じ道を往復する習慣に甘んじてしまいがちである。そしてスマートフォンの普及で、歩いているときでさえデジタルの世界に閉じこめられてしまう。画面とにらめっこをしているときは、周りでなにがおこっているか気づかないし、知りたいとも思わない。このノッティングヒル・ウォーキングガイドはデジタルの世界に閉じこもっているあなたを、今この場所にひき戻すために書かれた、いわばアイフォ

ン中毒の解毒剤のようなものである。

　これからご紹介する4つのウォーキングコースは、ノッティングヒルの多様な文化と歴史を肌で感じてもらうようにデザインされている。この地域は過去60年間に劇的に変化し、貧しいスラム地区からロンドンで最も高価な憧れの住宅街に大きく様変わりした。これらの4つのコースは、テーマに分けられたノッティングヒル近代史のスナップ写真集であり、ノッティングヒル・カーニバルの起源、ポートベロ・マーケットの発展、特筆すべき建物とその住人達、そして映画や音楽、書籍の中に再発見されたノッティングヒルの豊かな文化と有名人（ホークスウィンドからヒューグラントまで）を幅広く網羅している。

　近年の再開発の波は、この地域を表面的にきれいにしたが、たとえどんなにたくさんのお金が流れ込んできても、この地域独特の個性と魅力を変えることはできないだろう。『…ノッティングヒルのようなところは世界中どこにもない…』―GKチェスタトン

− ポートベロ・マーケット −

1, バーム・アンティーク Barham Antiques at 111 Portobello. 2, バージン・レコード本社 Virgin Records HQ, Vernon Yard Mews. 3, ポートベロ公団住宅 The Portbello Estate. 4, レッド・ライオン The Red Lion Arcade 165-169 Portobello Road. 5, タルボット通りとベルネムクレセントの交差点 Talbot Road/Blenheim Crescent. 6, ウエストウェイテント下の古着マーケット The Westway Canopy vintage market. 7, アックラム・ビレッジ・マーケット Acklam Village Market. 8, アイ・ワズ・ロード・キチュナーズ・バレット I Was Lord Kitchener's Valet, 293 Portobello Road. 9, ジョージ・フィッシュ・バー George's Fish Bar, 329 Portobello Road.

　ッティングヒルを探索する一番手っ取り早い
　　方法は、南端のノッティングヒル・ゲートから
北のゴルボーン通りまでまっすぐのびたこのポート
ベロ通りを歩いてみることである。魔法ように一夜
にして現れるたくさんの露店を見ながら、この西ロン
ドンの通りをご案内することにしよう。

　ポートベロ・マーケットは区画ごとにはっきりとし
た特徴と専門分野があり、例えば、ウェストウェイ高
架下には古着、ゴルボーン通りには食べ物屋台、そし
てウエストボーン・グローブからエルギン・クレセン
トの無数のアンティーク・アーケードには、骨董品や
ビンテージなどの逸品珍品があふれている。英国最
大のアンティーク蚤の市としても世界的に有名になっ
たポートベロ・マーケットには、毎週1000軒以上の露
店が並び、十万人以上のお客が集まる。それだけにマー
ケットのある週末はポートベロ通りのどこを歩くに
しても少々時間がかかる。見物人でごった返している
通りを、ウォーキングの快速で駆け抜けるのは至難
の業なので、最初からのんびり散歩すると割り切って
おくほうがいいだろう。昔から金曜と土曜はポートベ
ロ・マーケットが一番にぎわう日だが、最近は日曜日
も人気が高まっている。

Alice's Antiques（アリスのアンティーク）**86
Portobello Road** はこの辺では一番古い小道具屋
で、創業はポートベロ・マーケットが古物商の全盛期
だった頃にさかのぼる。近所にあるバーム・アンティ
ーク（**No.111**）とジュディ・フォックス（**No.81**）の店主

Alice's Antiques（アリスのアンティーク）

たちはその頃からの同朋で、配達を協力しあったり、お客に合う店を勧めあったり、古き良き時代の面影が今も店内に残っている。ポートベロ通りで古物商を営む人たちが急激に増えたのは、第二次世界大戦が終わるころだった。当時このあたりの賃貸料は安かったので、試しに露店から始めてみて、うまくいけばこの通りに店を構えることもできた。

Barham Antiques（バーム・アンティーク）**111 Portobello Road** もその例である。今は二代目のマイケル・バームが現在この店を切り盛りしているが、徴兵から引き上げた父親が1940年代後半に露店を始め、その商売がうまくいったので、1950年代初頭にここにあったウェールズ産の牛乳屋を買い取った。店内には骨董の茶入れ箱やウイスキー用クリスタルグラスと一緒に、きれいなマーケトリー(寄木細工)の木箱なども並んでいるから、ちょっと中をのぞいてみ

てはどうだろう。

　さらに北に向かって歩き、ウエストボーン・グローブとの交差点を渡ったら、聞き耳を立てながらあたりをちょっと見渡してみよう。バスカー（路上ミュージシャン）が演奏しているかもしれない。バスキング（路上ライブ）もポートベロで長く続く名物の一つで、今や時の人になってしまった歌手たちも、投げ銭用の帽子を地面に置き、ギター片手に歌っていた。例えばホークウィンドで有名になったデイブ・ブロック、最近ならポップグループのシュガーシスターズなんかは、今でも時々土曜日にやってきてそのきれいな歌声で観衆を和ませている。

　Vernon Yard mews（バーノン・ヤード・ミュー）**119 Portobello Road** をみてみよう。ポートベロ通りという名前は、英国海軍提督エドワード・バーノンに由来する。彼は1739年のジェンキスの耳戦争で中央アメリカのポルトベロ（現パナマ）をスペインから勝ち取った英雄だ。1970年代から80年代にかけてリチャード・ブロンソンのバージン・レコードがこの **2–4 Vernon Yard** に事務所を構えて、マイク・オルドフィールドの『チュブラ・ベル』やセックスピストルズの『勝手にしやがれ』などを次々と発表。バージン・レコードはロンドンで最先端のレコード会社になった。

　Portobello Court estate（ポートベロ公団住宅）は、1950年代にロンドン州議会の貧民街一掃政策の一環で建てられた。この区画にあった古いビクトリア様式の長屋は、取り壊され、今ある公共住宅に建て替えたのである。もしそのビクトリア様式の長屋がそ

のまま残っていたら、今人気のノッティングヒルの豪
邸として相当な資産価値になっていただろう。

　ポートベロ通りが平坦になっていくとその先に、
有名なアンティーク蚤の市のアーケードが見えてく
る。**The Red Lion Arcade** (レッドライオン) **No.165-
169**は地元の古物商人スーザン・ガースが1951年に開
業したロンドンで最初のアーケードと言われている。
実はそこには２つのブルー・プラーク(*注)が存在す
る。一つはスーザン・ガースが最初のアンティークショ
ップを開いた、もう一つは115番地のジューン・アイ
ルワードが最初だ、と記されている。どちらもまだ公
式に認定されていない。(*注 : Blue Plaqueイングリッ
シュ・ヘリテイジが管理する建物の歴史的なつながり
を伝えるために建物の外壁に設置される銘板)

　ポートベロ通りからウエストボーン・グローブ、チェ
プストウ・ビラ、エルギン・クレセントまでの一帯に約
10軒のアーケードがあり、蚤の市の時 (ふつうは金曜
日と土曜日) だけ開店する。アンティークやエフェメラ
の宝庫、そこはまさしくアラジンの魔法の洞窟だ。中
には80軒近い露店が収容されているアーケードもあ
り、そこには古い測量器具やアールヌーボーの花瓶、
ビンテージの時計など様々なものを売っている。こん
な素敵な場所にいると、夢中になってつい時間を忘れ
てしまう。

　さらに歩くと、次は青果露店が見えてくる。イモや
ニンジン、イチゴにバナナいろいろな野菜や果物が
山高く積まれ　八百屋のおじさんの威勢の良い掛け
声が聞こえてくる

Fruit and veg stalls（青果屋台）

　「あまーい国産イチゴ、ひとカゴたったのパアアアン（ド）！」

　そもそもポートベロ通りで青果露店が始まったのは、百年以上前、地域の貧しい住民たちに安くてまともな食料を供給するためだった。そしてこのマーケットは、これらの青果露店を基軸に成り立ってきたのだ。

　ここで家族代々商売をしている露店が、まだ少しだが残っている。彼らは役所が法的な出店許可証を発行する前、警察官の取り締まりをすり抜けながら露店をしてきた。オックスファム古本店 **No.170 Portobello Road** あたりに陣取っているシェリル・コリンズをさがしてみよう。シェリルはポートベロ・マーケットで露店を続ける家族の3代目で、この地域で最も顔見知りの多い店である。彼女の朝は3時半、ヒースロー近くの大きな青果市場に行くことから始まる。買い付けた野菜果物をトラックにつめこみ、8時半には

ここに到着しなくてはならない。しかし常連客は急速に減り続け、この１０年間で少なくとも100年以上代々続いた３つの露店商が姿を消してしまった。大型スーパーマーケットの台頭と地域の高級住宅化といった時代の流れに屈するしかなかったのだろう。

Talbot Road/ Portobello（タルボット通りの角あたり）、もし運が良ければそこの主人のピーター・ケインに会えるかもしれない。彼は元ミドル級プロボクシングのチャンピオンで、165回も試合出場の上、1972年ピエール・パウロ・パッソリニ監督の映画『カンタベリ物語』にも出演している露店商人である。ピーターの家族もまた代々続く露店商であった。祖母のドロシー・ケインは第一次世界大戦直後にここで商売を始めて、1920年代の終わり役所から正式な許可証を得た最初の露店である。二次大戦のときはドイツ軍の爆撃にかかわらず、空襲のときはブレネム・クレセントの避難所に隠れ、それが終わればすぐに通りに出てきて商売を始めた、という逸話が残っている。

20世紀の初めごろは **Talbot Road / Blenheim Crescent**（タルボット通りとブレナム・クレセントの交差点）は野外コンサートや政治デモの集会広場だった。貸し出されたバレル・オルガンでその日のおすすめ曲が演奏され、午後になると観衆はさらに膨れ上がり、見ているほうも飛び入りで演奏したり、最後には踊ったり歌ったりと盛り上がった。

Electric Cinema（エレクトリック・シネマ）**191 Portobello Road** もそんな大衆娯楽の発信源で、イ

The Electric Cinema（エレクトリック・シネマ）

ギリスでもっとも歴史の古い現役の映画館の一つである。1911年2月27日創業開始、設計は建築家ジェラルド・シーモア・バレンティン、詰めれば600人くらいの観客を収容できた。1台の映写機とオイルランプ、座席は固い木のベンチだったが、これはサイレント映画全盛のころの話なので、ほとんどの映画の上映時間は10分足らずだった。第一次世界大戦中には、ドイツ系のマネージャーが屋根から飛行船に秘密の暗号を発信しているといううわさが流れて、地元人たちが建物を襲撃したことが新聞の見出しとなった。

　1919年、時代に合わせてエレクトリックからインペリアルと改名し、古い映画を2本立て週3回入れ替え上映していた。1950年代ごろにはウエストボーン・グローブに新しくできた柔らかい椅子とのモダンな内装が売りのオデオン映画館との競合に負け、客足も減ってしまった。インペリアルはそのころから安い入場料でオールナイト上映するようになり、地元住民に

は「バグホール」（害虫の住みか）というあだ名で呼
ばれるようになった。

　1969年にはジョン・マックウィリアム率いる若い
実業家ヒッピーたちが、『エレクトリック・シネマ倶楽
部』と銘打って土曜の夜だけに映画館を借り切り、シ
ーズンごとにテーマを決めて、フィルム・ノワール、音
楽映画、ヤクザものやミュジカルなどのジャンルを次
々に上映していた。それが大当たりしてすぐさま終日
上映となり、しばらくの間イギリスの芸術的レパート
リー映画館の手本となった。ブリクストンのリッチー
やオックスフォードのプレイハウス、バーミンガムの
アーツ・ラボなど、当時の新鋭映画館も、その興業方
式を真似るようになる。

　エレクトリック映画館は現在ソーホーハウスに買
収され、オイルランプ、ベンチは姿を消した。その代
わりにできたバー・カウンターで注文したシャンパン
片手に、アーム・チェアー、ソファー、あるいはベッド
席で寝転んで、優雅に映画を鑑賞できるようになっ
ている。

The Grain Shop（グレインショップ）**269
Portobello Road**　はかつて、自然食品店の草分け的
存在の　**Ceres Grain Store**（セリース自然食材店）
があった場所である。創業者カリフォルニア出身のサ
ムス兄弟（グレゴリーとクレイグ）は、1968年にシード
というマクロビ自然食レストランをオープンしてイギ
リスでの自然食革命に火をつけた。ジョン・レノンと
オノ・ヨーコ、マーク・ボラム、ピーター・タウンゼン
などの有名人が常連客に顔を連ねるおしゃれな人気

スポットになった。そしてシード・レストランで食べた料理を家で作ってみたいというお客からの要望を受けて、1969年マクロビダイエットの基本食材を販売するセリース自然食料店がオープンしたのである。その後、併設のパン屋とカフェ、続いて出張サービスも始め、ワイト島フェスティバルや1971年の初回のグラストンブリー祭での自然食野外ケータリングを成功させた。

　ポートベロ通りを北上すると **Westway Canopy**（ウェストウェイ高架下の天蓋マーケット広場）にたどり着く。金曜日と土曜日はとりわけ古着屋台（ビンテージ・ショップ）一色である。この25年以上、ポートベロ・マーケットはスタイリスト、ファッションデザイナー、ミュージシャン、ブロガー、ファッション学生なら押さえておくべき場所となっている。とくに業界人の日といわれる金曜日は、ポール・スミス、ラルフ・ローレン、ドナ・キャランからジェイ・クルーといった主要ブランドメーカーのデザイナーがやってきては、デザインのアイデアになりそうなものをひとしきり買い付けて、ちょっといじってから自社のブランドタッグを付けて次のシーズンの新作として発表したりしている。屋台を歩いて商品をくまなく見ていくと、1970年代のブランド、バス・ストップ、ミス・マウス、オジー・クラークや、アメリカの軍服、レアなデニムブランドまで掘り出し物がいっぱいだ。ビンテージファッションのルーツを探ればたぶんポートベロにたどり着くだろうし、ここにはまだとっておきの掘り出し物が眠っている。

The Acklam Village Market（アックラム・ビレッジ・マーケット）は、ポートベロ通りを挟んで反対側のウェストウェイ高架下にある。ここではチーズ、焼き立てパン、カップケーキにオリーブまでいろんな食べ物を売っていて、中東、アフリカン、ドイツ、カリビアン、メキシカン、フレンチ、スペインなど各国料理の食べ歩きができる。

さらに北に向かって歩く前に、ちょっと時間を割いてみてほしいのは、**Falafel King**（ファラフェル・キング）**274 Portobello Road** の壁に描かれたバンクシーのグラフィティだ。イーゼルを片手にベレーをかぶった画家がバンクシー独特のスタイルで描かれている。保護プラスチックがかけられたそのグラフィティの上に落書されているのはやるせないが、ほとんどの観光客が、その壁に歴史が刻まれていることすら知らないのである。

そこからポートベロ通りを横切って**No.293**の前で止まってみよう。1966年そこは『 I Was Lord Kitchener's Valet（アイ・ワズ・ロード・キチュナーズ・バレット）』"という、スインギング・ロンドン時代にとりわけ粋なビンテージ・ブティックだった。オーナーのイアン・フィスクとジョン・ポールは、ポートベロ・マーケットで露店をした後、この店を構えてビクトリア時代のビンテージの軍服とアクセサリー、古いガラクタ類を専門に販売していた。1966年5月27日金曜日、ローリングストーンズのリードシンガー、ミック・ジャガーがいきなり入って、店内の服をひとしきり品定めした後グレナディア軍隊の真紅のジャケットを試着した。

　その夜に放映されたＴＶ番組『ポップ・オブ・ザ・ポップス』でローリングストーンズは『プレイ・ウィズ・ファイヤー』を歌った。そしてなんとミック・ジャガーはその時、例のジャケットを着ていたのだ。その翌日、店の前にはミックのファッションを真似したい若いファンがたくさん詰めかけて大行列ができ、その日中に店内の在庫はすべて売り切れてしまったのである。それをきっかけに、クリームのエリック・クラプトンやジミ・ヘンドリックスなど、当時活躍していたほかのロック・スターの間でもミリタリー・ルックが大いに流行した。

　1年後の1967年の後半、ポップアーティストのピーター・ブレイクがこの店の前を歩いていた時に、ビートルズのアルバム、『サージェント・ペッパーズ・ロンリー・ハーツ・クラブ・バンド』のスタイリングのアイデアがひらめいたといわれている。その後も軍服はファッション史上受け継がれ、アメリカのファッションデザイナー、マーク・ジェイコブスが2002年にアレンジしたミリタリー・ルックを発表しているし、ギャップやプライマークなどのアパレルチェーン店も時折ミリタリー調デザインの服を出している。

　その真向かいに、ロンドンで最も優れた個人経営レコードショップ、**Honest Jon's Records**（オネスト・ジョン・レコード）**278 Portobello**　がある。1974年創業したその店は、ジャズ、ブルース、レゲエ、ダンス、フォーク、のほか、アウターナショナルサウンドなども専門に扱っている。お得意さんの一人に、あの有名なデーモン・アルバン（ブラーとゴリラズのリード・

シンガー）がいる。彼はお店のことを、「僕が音楽の
方向性を学んだ教育の現場」と説明している。実際、
デーモンは店の経営者とあまりに気が合ったものだ
から、一緒にレコード会社をたちあげている。発表し
たいくつかのアルバムの中には第二次大戦後の初期
のロンドン黒人音楽を発掘して再編集した『ロンドン
は私の場所』と呼ばれるコンピレーションアルバム（
編集盤）がある。

　最終地点までさらにポートベロを北向きに歩こう。
ラディントン通りをわたると、フリー・マーケットスタ
イルの露店が目立つようになってくる。ほとんどの観
光客はここが最後だと思って引き返すのだが、このま
ま歩き続けてゴルボーン通りを見て行くことをお勧め
する。ここにはおいしい食べ物屋台のほかに、折衷
スタイルのビンテージ家具屋や素敵なカフェが点在
している。**George's Fish Bar**（ジョージ・フィッシュバ
ー）**329 Portobello Road**のフィッシュアンドチップス
は住民のお気に入りだ。

ウォーク2

ー ノッティングヒル・カーニバル ー

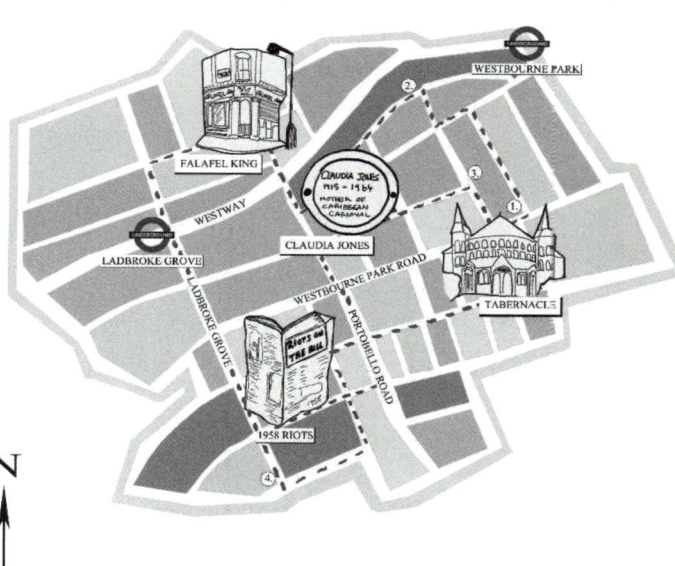

1，ロンドン・フリースクール The London Free School, 26 Powis Terrace. 2，ラウンの保育園 Rhaune Laslett's Nursery, 34 Travistock Cresent. 3，マングローブ・レストラン The Mangrove Restaurant, 8 All Saints Road. 4，エルギン・クレセントとラッドブローク・グローブの交差点 Corner of Elgin Crescent and Ladbroke Grove.

毎年恒例のノッティングヒル・カーニバルは西ヨーロッパで最大規模のストリート・パーティだそうだ。月曜が祝日になる8月末の週末には、150万人近い見物人が集まってくる。普段は閑静な住宅街の様相をしたノッティングヒルの通りが、一転してパーティのメッカに早変わりし、レゲエ、ダブ、サルサなどのライブ・ミュージックに、37台のスタティック・サウンドシステム、ソカ山車、スチールバン・バンド、仮装行列がラッドブロック・グローブを巡行する。カーニバルは、ここで共生してきた文化と民族の多様性の祭典である。次のウォーキングでは、ノッティングヒル・カーニバルを現在のものに形づける重要な役割を担った先駆者たちをご紹介しよう。問題の火種を抱えてひっそりと始まったカーニバルが、いまや世界的に有名なイベントになったことは、いろいろな意味でこの地域の歴史を映し出しているのかもしれない。

2016年、カーニバルは誕生50周年を迎えた。このウォークの出発点は、**No.9 Blenheim Crescent**（ブレネム・クレセント）。おしゃれなブティックや個性的なお店が並んでいるこの通りでは、ひどくみすぼらしい外観の建物だ。しかし、ここは1958年9月1日、およそ300人の黒人男性集団が、テディボーイとよばれた不良少年グループを含む地元の白人男性集団と衝突、戦後最悪の人種間暴動が勃発した、あの場所なのである。

その当時9番地はトトバッグ・カフェと呼ばれ、西インド諸島からの移民してきたばかりの新顔の黒人

たちが集い、煙草をふかしたり酒を飲んだり、ドミノ
を楽しんだり情報交換をする場所になっていた。初
代のDJミキサー、キング・ディックやバロン・バッカー

カウント・サックルが選んだ黒人音楽がバックミュ
ージックにながれるその店は、ちょっと果敢なボヘミ
ア志向の白人客にも好まれていた。たとえば、小説
家コリン・マッキネス、音楽家のジョージー・フェイ
ム、時には上流階級のウィンストン・チャーチルの末
娘セーラ・チャーチルの姿もあったそうだ。しかしそ
の8月末の蒸し暑い夕暮れには、黒人と白人の関係
はもうすでに対立が避けられないほど悪化していた
から、誰もその店で社交する気分にはならなかった
だろう。

西インド諸島の移民からなる黒人コミュニティと
白人のコミュニティとの緊張関係は数か月の間に徐
々にひどくなっていった。この地域に台頭していた白
人中心主義の先導グループ、オズワルド・モズリーの
率いるネオ・ファシスト組織、ユニオン・ムーブメン
トと、コリン・ジョーダン率いるホワイト・ディフェン
ス・リーグ　が白人グループを煽動し、人種間対立を
あおりたてていた。(コリン・ジョーダンはホランドパー
ク近くのプリンスデール通りに住んでいた)。そし
てその週末起こる暴動のきっかけは、金曜日の夜に
起こったある痴話げんかだった。地下鉄ラティマー
駅から出てきたジャマイカ人の黒人男性とスエーデ
ン人の白人女性の夫婦が罵り合いのひどい喧嘩をし
ていた。近くにいた白人グループが止めに入ったとこ
ろが、逆に黒人男性ともみあいになってしまったので
ある。

「右の頬を殴られたら左の頬を出してやりなさい」
という聖書の教えどおり、黒人コミュニティは数か月
もの間その挑発を我慢強く無視をしつづけていた。
しかしそのたった一週間前にも白人不良集団（テディ
ボーイ）が徒党を組み、「黒人狩り」と称して町の中
を徘徊し、その結果6人が病院に運ばれ、黒人の住
む家や店の窓ガラスは壊され放火された。だから8月
31日月曜日、黒人コミュニティの我慢は限界に達して
いたのである。

　トトバッグ・カフェには、その日の朝早くから黒人
男たちが集まり、おもいおもいに、肉切り包丁、火炎
瓶、ナイフ、身の回りにある武器になりそうなものを
持ち込んだ。昼過ぎになるとさらに多くの黒人男たち
が店内に集まった。同時に白人集団も外の通りに群
れだし「黒人をあぶりだせ！」という挑発的なヤジリ
声が聞こえはじめた。そして午後6時を少し回ったと
き、トトバッグ・カフェの二階の窓が開け放たれ、レン
ガやらガラス瓶やらが次々と白人暴徒に向けて投げ
つけられた。そして表通りでは2つの集団の暴力闘
争が始まったのである。サイレンをけたたましく鳴ら
し6台の黒い護送車で警察が駆け付けた時には、テ
ディボーイ、黒人に交じって、新聞記者たちもその暴
動の混乱に巻き込まれていた。幸い死者を出すこと
なく暴動は収まり、群衆も散り散りに消えていった。
そしてノッティングヒル暴動は、翌朝の朝刊の大見出
しになったのである。

　タビストック・スクエアにあるベース・カット美容室
252 Portobello Road and Tavistock Road（ポートベ

Blue Plaque of Claudia Jones
（クローディア・ジョーンズの銘板）

ロ通りとタビストック通り）の壁の上のほうにブルー・プラークがありこのように記されている。「クローディア・ジョーンズ1915－1964　英国のカリビアン・カーニバルの生みの親。1958年8月バンクホリデーのノッティングヒル暴動に対する地域の対応として1959年1月から毎年恒例のカーニバルを開催する」。クローディアはその週末の惨事を目撃し、その対立を緩和するためになにか手を打たなくてはならないと真剣に考えた。

　彼女は本当にすごい女性だった。トリニダディアン・トバゴで生まれ米国で育ったが、マッカーサー時代にコミュニスト政党を支援したために国外追放されてしまい移民として、ロンドンに流れつく。英国初の黒人新聞『ウェストインディアン・ガゼット』を設立した活動家でもあった。その週末にノッティングヒルで起こった悲惨な暴力事件を目撃したクローディ

アは、（同じ週末にノッティンガムで起こった暴動の
ニュースを新聞で読んでいた）地元の黒人コミュニ
ティのリーダーたちとの話し合い、そこでカリビアン文
化の素晴らしさを披露しようというカーニバルのアイ
デアが生まれたのである。

　まず1959年に最初の室内カーニバルが開催され
た。翌年から以後4年間、カーニバル参加者は増え
続け、そして1962年、メリルボーンのセイモアホール
で開催された、ビューティコンテスト、カリプソ音楽
とリンボー・ダンスなどの出し物を含んだイベントに
は、なんと2000人もの参加者が集まったのである。ク
ローディアが主催した室内カーニバルは、1964年の
クリスマスイブ、彼女の早すぎる死によって中断して
しまうのだが、その後も、クローディア・ジョーンズは
英国のカリビアン・カーニバルの生みの親と評価さ
れている。

　カーニバルは次の段階に進展する。セント・ルー
クス通りから角を曲がって **26 Powis Terrace**（ポウィ
ス・テラス）に行くことにしよう。ここは1966年、写真
家、ジャーナリスト、政治活動家だったジョン・ホッ
ピー・ホプキンスの率いるロンドン・フリースクール
の活動拠点で、革新派の随筆家、ジョン・ミチェルが
無料で自宅の地下室を提供した。ホッピーは当時U
FOクラブの創設にも携わっていた地元の主要人物
で、アメリカを旅行した時に現地のフリー大学運動に
共鳴し、ロンドン・フリースクールを地域主体の生涯
教育プロジェクトにすることを構想し、写真、文学や
麻薬などあらゆる分野を学ぶ教室や、法律相談、地

元新聞の発行などの活動計画が話し合われていた。そんなロンドン・フリースクールの会合に、地元の活動家で運営実行派のラウン・ラスレットが参加したのである。

　ラウン・ランスレットは **34 Tavistock Crescent**（トラビストック・クレセント）（＊注この住所は現存しない）の自宅で、庭に遊技場を作り、保育所を運営していた。アメリカインディアンとロシア人家系の看護婦だったラウンは、1950年代終わりごろこの地域に移住してきたが、世話好きで、同志をまとめるのが大変うまく、地元の主要人物としても人望が厚かった。だからこそ、1966年5月、世界ヘビー級プロボクサー、モハメド・アリがヘンリー・クーパーと対戦するためにロンドンに来ていたときに、彼女の保育園にふらっと立ち寄り、子供たちに本を読み聞かせ、そこでファンと一緒に記念撮影をしたのである。

　ラウンはロンドン・フリースクールの実行グループと協力して、1966年9月18日から25日までの一週間ノッティングヒル祭という野外イベントを企画開催した。これはまさに地域住民全員が一丸となった努力の成果だった。工務店から借りたダンプカーは即席のステージに飾り付けられ、貸衣装屋がイベント用のコスチュームを寄贈し、持ち寄った食べ物や飲み物を取りまとめて、参加者全員にくまなく配分された。仮装行列で始まり、夜はオールセイント教会の集会場で、詩の朗読会、音楽と踊りなどが盛り込まれたそのイベントは大成功に終わった。ノッティングヒル祭は毎年恒例のお祭りとして、ラウンと夫のジムが1970年まで主催し、そのあと地域の人たちに引き継

がれた。タビストック・スクエアとポートベロ通りの交
差点にはそんなラウンの偉業をたたえたブルー・プ
ラークがある。

　1960年代後半から1970年代初期にかけてのカー
ニバルは、たった１つのスチールパン・バンドとダンス
（通称ジャンプ・アップ）に3000人ほどが参加する小
規模なものだったので、次のカーニバルの改革者が
出現する1973年まではイベント自体が消滅する危険
さえあった。レズリー・パーマーは、この地区出身の
若い教師で、1973年から1975年までのカーニバルを
主導した。現在のフェスティバルの構成要素としてな
じみ深い、スタスティック・サウンドシステム、マスカ
レードバンド、スポンサーから寄付金やラジオでの
生中継などを取り入れ、現在のカーニバル運営の基
礎を確立したのである。

All Saints Road（オールセイント通り）には、こ
の地区で一番古いレコード屋、**People's sound**（ピー
プルズ・サウンド）No.11 や、その隣に **Portobello
Music**（ポートベロ・ミュージック）**No.13** がある。そ
して1992年まで **The Mangrove Restaurant**（マング
ローブ・レストラン）**No.8** があった。

　マングローブは当時のカーニバルの活動の事実
上の本拠地で、見物客15万人という新記録を達成し
ようとしていた。ウエストボーン・パーク通りでエル・
リオというカフェをやっていたフランク・クリッチロ
ーが、1968年、ここにマングローブをオープンした。
エル・リオといえば1963年のプロヒューモ事件のさ
なか、スティーブン・ウォードとクリスティン・キーラ

ーの密会場所として新聞の一面を騒がせた、あのいわくつきのカフェである。マングローブも開店後すぐに評判となり、黒人たちのたまり場となったが、そこには少なからず白人の革新主義者や文化人ボヘミアンの常連もふくまれていた。ミュージシャンのジミ・ヘンドリックス、女優のバネッサ・レッドグレイブ、ボブ・マーリやニナ・シーモンなどがよくそこに寄り集まっていたようだ。常に何かにつけて話題の中心だったマングローブ・レストランの地下室では、定期刊行のコミュニティ新聞『ハスラー』が刷られていた。

　ノッティングヒル・カーニバルのある週は土曜日の夕方から、オールセイント通り全体がマングローブ・スチールパン・バンドの練習場になるので、ぜひ行ってみてほしい。素晴らしい響きがお祭気分をさらに盛り上げてくれることだろう。

　ノッティングヒル・カーニバルはいつも順調に進展したわけではなかった。1970年後半から80年代にかけては何度かトラブルがあったので、カーニバルの存続自体が疑問視されていた。ポートベロ通りに戻り、北向きにあるいてウェストウェイ高架下をくぐったところにある **Falafel King**（ファラフェル・キング）**274 Portobello Road** のドアの前は1976年のカーニバル史上最悪の暴動が発生した場所である。

　その年のフェスティバル参加者によると、ウェストゲイトの下からこの場所に向かって、警官が見物客の黒人のグループを追いかけているのを見た、そしてある時点で黒人群衆は自分たちが警官よりも優勢だと気付いたので反撃し始めた、ということのようだ。続

いて火事場泥棒や乱闘がそこかしこで起こり、店の
ガラスが粉々に割られ、車はボコボコにされ、家々が
放火された。100人以上の警官がけが、60人以上の市
民が負傷し、そのうちの何人かは重傷であった。警
察は66人の男たち（ほとんどが黒人）を逮捕したが、
次の公判で起訴されたのはたった17人、そのうち有
罪になったのはたった2人だけであった。

　その日に発生した暴動は、警官の強引な取り締ま
りに問題があったという見方が一般的になってい
る。暴動の前年、比較的平和なカーニバルでは、警
官動員数は300人足らずだったが、暴動のあった年に
は、その10倍近いおよそ3000人の警察官が動員され
た。平和を保つため、護衛バスを送りつけたのだ！ス
トップアンドサーチ法の対する反発、人種間の緊張
関係もピークに達していたので、暴力を扇動するのは
簡単だった。「群衆にはスリがいる」という警備名目
は、警察が見物客を威嚇し、殴るための言い訳に過
ぎなかった。

　その日の暴動に巻き込まれた2人の若い白人男
性は、ザ・クラッシュのジョー・ストラマーとポール・
シムノンだった。そのまま通りを横切って **Ladbroke
Grove**（ラッドブロック・グローブ）と **Elgin
Crescent**（エルギン・クレセント）の交差点に立って
みよう。そこがちょうど白人のパンクたち（反抗的な
若者の呼び名）がちょうどその日に居合わせた場所
になる。その日の経験がもとになってできたのが、衝
撃のデビューシングル『ホワイト・ライオット（邦題：
白い暴動＊注）』（＊注：正確には『白人たちの暴動』
）。その曲は翌年の5月にデビューアルバムでリリース

され、いまもなおロンドンパンクの典型的な曲となっている。

Tabernacle（ターバナックル）**34-35 Powis Square**
でこのウォーキングを終えることにしよう。通りから
少し奥まったところに位置するこの建物は、1887年
に建てられ、曲線の美しいロマネスク調の赤レンガ
の外壁と、入り口を挟んで両端にある低い筒状の塔
が特徴だ。現在のターバナックルは映画館併設のア
ート・コミュニティ・センターで、マングローブ・レスト
ランの後を引き継いでカーニバル・ビレッジとして運
営活動本部にもなっている。
　もしカーニバルの始まるころなら、奥にあるパン・
ルームでよくマングローブ・スチールパン・バンドが練

Tabernacle（ターバナックル）

習しているから、運が良ければ演奏が聴けるかもしれない。バー・カウンターの横にある常設展示スペースには、過去50年の象徴的なカーニバルの写真の数々が展示されているし、カフェのメニューでは、イングリッシュ・ブレックファーストとカリビアン・羊肉カレーとプランテン・チップスなどがおすすめだ。

ウォーク 3

− 音楽・文学・映画 −

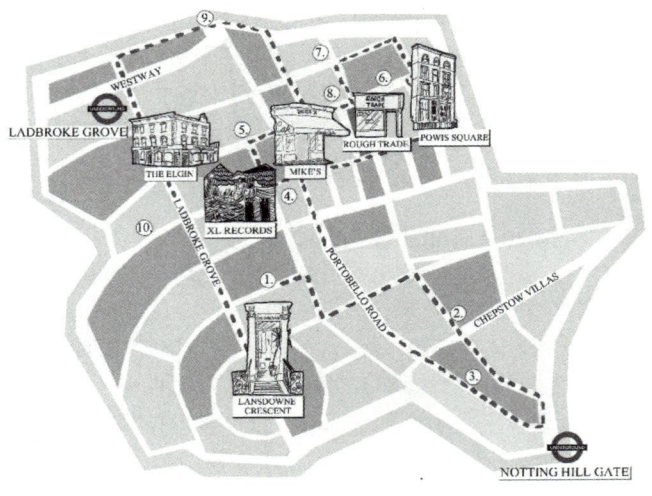

1，ジョー・ミーク録音スタジオ　Joe Meek's home recording studio, 20 Arundel Garden. 2，作家たちの家　Literary House, 24 Chepstow Villas. 3，ジョージ・オーウェル下宿　George Orwell's lodgings, 22 Portobello Road. 4，トラベル・ブックショップ　The Travel Bookshop, 13 Blenheim Crescent. 5，青い扉　The Blue Door, 280 Westbourne Park Road. 6，オールセイント教会　All Saints Church. 7，アイランド・レコード　Island Records Studios, 8-10 Basing Street. 8，『ハード・デイス・ナイト』映画ロケ地　Scene in *A Hard Day's Night*, 20 All Saints Road. 9，フレンズ本社　Frendz HQ 307 Portobello Road. 10，マーク・ボランの家　Marc Bolan's flat, 57 Blenheim Crescent.

このウォーキングは映画や音楽や文学に関係する場所、レコーディングスタジオから映画のロケ先、アングラ出版局などを紹介する。ノッティングヒルは今でこそおしゃれな高級住宅地だが、1960年代から70年代には、言わずと知れたカウンター・カルチャー（*注）の中心だった。レゲエ、ロック、パンク、サイケデリック、ハードロック、フォーク、ダブなどあらゆる分野の音楽がこの細い通りからあふれだしていた。（*注：Counter cultureヒッピーやロック音楽を中心にした若者の対抗文化）

No.20 Arundel Gardens（アルンデル・ガーデン）には、初代ロックンロールの主要人物、傍若無人の音楽プロディーサー、ジョー・ミークの最初のホーム・スタジオがあった。ミークは1962年の12月に発表されるや否や世界的に大ヒットした楽曲『テルスター』をプロデュースしたことでよく知られているが、それがマーガレット・サッチャー首相のお気に入りの曲だったことも有名だ。そのレコードの中で使われているホンキー・トンク・ピアノは、ポートベロ蚤の市で見つけてきたものである。

ミークは1957年にここの一階の小さなワンルームの部屋を借りて、オープンリールデッキ、エコー・ユニット、マイク、アンプなどを詰め込み、まるでエキセントリックな科学者が出てくるB級映画を彷彿させるかの如く、床には数えきれないほどの電気コードが重なり合っていた。演奏者や音楽プロデユーサーが自宅にホーム・スタジオの類を持つことは、今ではそう珍しいことでもないが、1950年当時はまさに前代

未聞だった。そういう意味でミークは先駆者だった
が、彼の賃貸契約は短期間で終わってしまう。彼が
プロデュースしたスキッフル音楽、ジミー・ミラーの『
シズリング・ホット』のレコード販売を記念したバー
ベキュー・パーティに150人くらいの客が集まり、収拾
がつかなくなってしまった。近所の住民たちはこれ
には相当辟易したようで、その直後、ミックは立ち退
き勧告されてしまったのである。

ロックンロールやスキッフルといった音楽が毎日
のようにラジオから流れていた1950年代後半、一方
で『怒れる若者たち（アングリー・ヤングメン）』と呼
ばれる劇作家や小説家グループが文壇をにぎわせて
いた。その主要メンバーがノッティングヒルの家に住
んでいたのである。

少し勾配のある坂道を上がると **No.24 Chepstow
Villas** （チェプストウ・ビラ）がある。現在ならロン
ドンの富裕層が住む、典型的な純白外壁のノッティ
ングヒル邸宅であるが、時計を1950年代に逆戻りに
すると、そこには全く違う風貌の家と、全く毛色の違
う人住民たちの姿があっただろう。当時このあたり
は、廃墟が立ち並ぶ雑居地区だった。多くの家の窓
枠は腐り、白い外壁は剥がれ落ち、庭は荒れ放題だ
った。

1950年か1960年代にこの家を訪れたら、家の中は
きっと物書きや絵描きの集会場のような雰囲気だっ
ただろうし、実際、作家や画家や俳優が入れ代わり
立ち代わりこの家に住んでいた。この家は、暖炉つ
き、天井の高い8つの部屋に仕切られて、かび臭い

Chepstow Villas（チェプストウ・ビラ）

地下室には少しの間だが作家のディラン・トーマスも
住んでいたのではないかとうわさされている。当時の
郵便屋が配達した手紙の宛先名には、たとえばカル

ト作家で麻薬常習のアレクサンダー・トロッキーや、スコットランド人２人組画家のコフーンとマックブライド、ウェールズ人小説家でジャーナリストのビル・ホプキンス、小説家のクレシダ・リンジー、画家のジョネルビスとロナルド・ジェイビス、俳優のダドリー・サットンなどの名前が含まれていたようだ。1956年、少しの期間だったが、最も有名なのがコリン・ウイルソンである。処女作『アウトサイダー』で、彼は一夜にして衝撃の文壇デビューを果たした。その翌年に発行された期待の次作『宗教と反抗人』で、多くの批判を浴び、彼は傷心のあまり、自分の借りていた部屋を同じ地区に住んでいた新生作家ローラ・デル・リヴォに明け渡して、コーンウォールに引きこもってしまった。

　デル・リヴォは今もこの辺に住んでいる。もう８０歳代のおばあちゃんだが、毎週金曜と土曜日にはウェストウェイ高架下で靴下なんかを売っている。彼女はそのボヘミアな家の最後の生き証人だ。彼女はその家に引っ越してからいくつかの小説を書いたが、最初の作，『 The Furnished Room（ザ・ファーニッシュド・ルーム）』はダイアナ・ドース主演　マイケル・ウィナー監督で1963年に映画化され、『西のイレブン』という邦題で日本でも上映もされている。ノッティングヒル界隈をロケ先に、少しさびれたボヘミアの雰囲気をうまく映し出しているモノクロ映画である。

　チェスプトウ・ビラからポートベロ通りまで戻り、南に向かって **No.22 Portobello Road**（ポートベロ通り）、ここは1927年の冬、ジョージ・オーウェルとい

う名前で有名な、　24歳の若い新鋭の小説家エリック・ブレアが居候していた家である。彼はビルマのインド帝国警察の警視長の職を辞して、妻と幼児を連れてイギリスに引き上げた。風が吹き抜ける最上階の小さな部屋は、灯り取りのろうそくでひとしきり手を温めなくては字が書けなかったほど寒かった。そんな粗悪な住環境にもかかわらず、エリックはあの『パリ・ロンドン放浪記』の一部をこの家で書き上げ、小説家としての道が開かれた。あとは文学史に記されたとおりである。あれから22番地の家の住環境は改善されたようだ。2014年にこの家が売りに出された時には250万ポンドの売値がついたのだから。

　ポートベロ通りを北に戻ると、アンティークショップに埋め尽くされた一角にたどり着く。この辺りは1968年にディック・クレメント監督映画、『オットレイ』の撮影ロケ現場である。興行としては失敗だったが、スウィンギング・ロンドンを舞台にしたこの犯罪スパイ映画の冒頭シーンは料金を払ってでもみる価値はある。主演俳優のトム・コートニーが、よく晴れた日のポートベロ通りを闊歩するあの場面だ。コートニー演じる主役、うだつの上がらない悲運の骨董屋が、顔見知りの店員や露店の友人にきさくにあいさつを交わしながら歩いていく、その場面に出てくるポートベロ通りの風景は、今とほとんど変わらない。
　ポートベロ通りを世界的に広めたのは、その　30年後、同じようにポートベロ・マーケットを背景に撮影され、大ヒットした超有名映画だった。ヒュー・グラントとジュリア・ロバーツ主演『ノッティングヒルの

恋人』は、ノッティングヒルのロケ地めぐりという観光アトラクションを生みだした。そして世界中からやって来るファンが、今も映画に出てくるお店を突きとめたり、あの青色のドアの前で記念撮影をしたりしている。

　ポートベロ通りを歩いて、**Blenheim Crescent**（ブレネム・クレセント)との交差点を左にまがると、**The Notting Hill Bookshop**（ノッティングヒル・ブックショップ）**13 Blenheim Crescent** がある。ここには元々、個人経営のトラベル・ブックショップという本屋があり、この映画の監修にも携わった脚本家リチャード・カーティスが『ノッティングヒルの恋人』の中で描いた架空の『トラベル・ブック・カンパニー』のモデルになっている。僕は実際その本屋で何年か働いていたが、賃貸料や事業税が引き上げられ、オンラインショップの追い打ちを食らって経営が行き詰まった。しかし新しいオーナーは本屋を継続し、内装も元のままだから、店中に入ってあの映画のあのシーンに今も浸ることができる。

　青色のドアはもう一本北側の通りの交差点、**No.280 Westbourne Park Road**（ウエストボーン・パーク通り)にある。この玄関ドアは、ノッティングヒルで最も象徴的で有名である。ヒュー・グラントの演じる気弱な書店店主ウイリアム・タッカーが住んでいて、俳優のリス・エヴァンス演じる同居人スパイクが、世界中の報道陣の前で、かっこいいグレーのブリーフ一丁でポーズを決めた、あの有名なシーン、あの場所だ。その家がロケ場として選ばれた理由は、映画

撮影当時、そこがリチャード・カーティス自身の自宅だったからである。その青色のドアは競売にかけられ、売上金は寄付された。現在の住人が新しい扉を青い色に塗ってくれたおかげで、観光客の記念撮影は今も続いている。

Mike's Café（マイクのカフェ）　**12 Blenheim Crescent** に逆戻りして、次のウォーキングの場所に向かう前に、コーヒーか軽く食事で一服しよう。マイクのカフェは1962年に創業して以来、フライアップ（イギリスの庶民的朝ごはん）を提供してきた。店内はトラフィックの1971年発表のアルバム、『ウェルカム・トゥー・ザ・キャンティーン』のジャケットにも登場する、今もなお地元民や観光客らしき人たちに人気の店だが、マイクのカフェはこの地区の再開発（ジェントリフィケーション）の波にじっと抵抗している。ちょうど成金投資家の前で堂々と座りこんで仕事をしている露店主のように…。

さらに歩いて、ポートベロ通りを渡り、ブレネム・クレセントの西側に入ると、伝説のレコード店、**Rough Trade Records**（ラフ・トレード）　**130 Talbot Road** がある。ラフ・トレードは1976年、ここから遠くないケンジントンパーク通りで創業した。1976年といえばちょうどパンクミュージックが大ブレイクした年である。このレコード店はすぐにパンク革命の発信源となり、パンク仲間の活動拠点になった。店内ではコピー機でライブポスターを刷ったり、同人誌を作ったり、店内の至る所にライブ告知のポスター貼られ、宣伝用チ

Rough Trade（ラフ・トレード）

ラシが配られた。同じ趣向の音楽マニアたちがこの
交流の場所に集まったことは、大変有意義だった。ラ
フ・トレードはケンブリッジ大学卒のきれいな天然パー
マのジェフ・トラビスが創業し、店の開店後すぐに
ラフトレード・レコード販売店とラフトレード・レコー
ド制作会社に拡大した。トラビスは制作会社のほう
に力を入れ始めたので、1982年にスタッフが販売店
を買い現在の住所に移転した。レコード制作会社の
方は80年代のサ・スミス、リバーティン、新世紀に入
ってザ・ストークなど、たくさんの将来性のあるバンド
と契約した。今もこの地域で活動を続けていて66番
地ゴルボーン通りに事務所がある。レコード販売店
のほうも大成功で、現在東ロンドンとニューヨークに
支店がある。

　タルボット通りを東に向かうと　**All Saints Church**（

オール・セイント教会)がある。1850年代に建てられたビクトリア朝ゴシック様式の教会である。だが建築主のサミュエル・ウォーカー牧師が倒産したため、建物は未完成のままで10年ほど放置された。そこにはジプシー達のキャンプ地と化し、地元民からはオール・シナーズ(*注)というニックネームで呼ばれていた。

　(*注：All Saints　(すべての聖人)と　All Sinners (すべての罪人)の語呂あわせ)

　1970年代まで、教会の隣側には、地味で目立たない小さな集会場があった。現在は不細工なレンガ造りの老人ホームが建っているが、その場所はまさしくロンドンのカウンター・カルチャー史上最も重要な場所である。1966年9月30日、ピンクフロイドはここで定期ライブ公演を始めた。それまでリズム＆ブルース系のカバーバンドだったピンクフロイドが、本格的なサイケデリックバンドに変貌し完全開花したのだ。

　そのライブ公演は、ピーター・ジェナーとアンドリュー・キングという2人の新顔のイベントマネージャーが企画運営したが、どちらも牧師の息子だったので、教会の集会場なら安く簡単に借りられるということを知っていた。しかもこの教会は、最も前衛的で刺激的なロンドンの中心にある。そのライブ契約は間違いではなかったにしろ、おそらくピンクフロイドだって、まさか教会の集会所でライブ演奏するとは考えたことがなかっただろう。誰が見てもこの教会の集会場はライブ会場としてはあまりにも質素だった。収容客数は多くて300人くらい、高い天井、きれいに清掃された板張りの床、その片隅の低い舞台の仮設の

ステージ…。しかしふたを開けてみると、内装なんて
どうでもよかった。初日には集会場の前に長蛇の列
ができ、定期ライブは大成功だったのである。

　その定期ライブの期間中、イルミネーションが初め
て導入された。いろいろな色のスポットライトを、演
奏中のピンクフロイドにあて、心理的トランス効果を
融合しよういう試みだった。「サイケな女子学生」と
呼ばれていたエミリー・ヤングは、すべてのライブコ
ンサートに通うほどバンドに入れ込んで、いつも音楽
に合わせてゆっくり渦を巻くように踊っていた。1967
年春に発表された2枚目のシングル『シー・エミリー・
プレイ』はピンクフロイドのリーダー、シド・バレット
がそんなエミリーを曲にしたものである。

　この定期ライブは12月に終了したが、トッテナム・
コート通りのクラブで、ＵＦＯと呼ばれる夜のライブ
公演イベントが始まったのはこの教会ホールでのライ
ブの成果でもあった。ロンドンで超おしゃれスポット
として、演奏者にも観客にも大いに話題となり、10か
月のイベント期間中、ジミ・ヘンドリックスや、ソフト
マシーン、もちろんピンクフロイドも、そこで演奏した
のだった。

　そこから西に歩くと、**Powis Square** （ポウィス・ス
クエア）がある。まさしくここは地元のロックなスポ
ットとして一番話題になった場所だろう。最初に見え
るのが角にある **No.25 Powis Square**、ドナルド・キ
ャメルとニック・ローグ監督の伝説的映画、『パフォ
ーマンス　青春の罠』の主人公、引退したロック・ス
ター、ターナーの家だ。この映画は今でこそカルトム

ービーの典型として映画学校の教科書になっている
が、配給会社ワーナーブラザーズでは、ほとんど放
映されないままお蔵入りした映画である。ロンドンの
超暴力的やくざのアングラな世界と、麻薬漬けのロッ
クンロール歌手の世界を融合させて、サイコ・スリラ
ーとして仕上げられた映画だが、不快で観るに堪え
ないシーンの多い問題作でもあった。

　学生や労働者たちが、パリとロンドンでバリケード
を組んでいた1968年の夏に撮影されたこの映画に
は、時代の混乱と喧騒の雰囲気がみごとに映し出さ
れた。そして、ミック・ジャガーがキース・リチャード
の恋人のアニタ・パレンバーグといちゃついていた撮
影現場では、麻薬疑惑や駆け引き、嫉妬の光景が、
映画の一シーンとして時にはプライベートとしても演
じきられ、タブロイド新聞をにぎわせていた。一方、
頭にきていたキース・リチャードは毎日ロケ先の外に
自分のベントレーを乗り付けて、撮影が終わるのを
じっと待ち、その日の撮影が終わるやアニタを現場
から引っ張り出して連れて帰っていた、という逸話も
ある。ボヘミアンな隠れ家に潜むやくざ、チャスを演
じたジェームズ・フォックスはあまりにもその役には
まり込んだものだから、精神的におかしくなって、映
画の撮影後芸能界に復帰するのに10年以上かかっ
たそうだ。

　出来上がった映画はあまり暴力的で鑑賞に堪え
なかったため、配給会社ワーナーブラザーズは対応
に苦慮したようだが、大幅に編集されたものが1970
年にようやく公開された。家の内装はナイツブリッジ
のアパートメントで撮影されたものの、（25番地ポウ

ィス・スクエアの家はカメラとライトを持ち込むには
小さすぎた）映画はその当時の荒廃したノッティング
ヒルの雰囲気をうまく映し出していた。

　余談になるが、ミック・ジャガーのバンド仲間で、
ローリングストーンズのリーダーだった、ブライアン・
ジョーンズも1962年から **No.18 Powis Square** に住
んでいたが、1968までにターナーのようなちょっと問
題のある男に変わってしまっていた。そして1969年の
7月の真夏の暑い夜、イギリス南部の自宅のプールで
真夜中の水泳をした後、彼は謎めいた状況で溺死し
てしまうのである。

　次に **8-10 Basing Street**（ベイジング・ストリート）
、最近までこの辺で一番有名なレコーディングスタ
ジオがあったところだ。**Island Records**（アイランド
レコード）は1969年にここにあった古い教会を買っ
て1970年1月にスタジオとしてオープンした。イーグ
ルス、レッドチェッペリン、ジェトロ・タル、ボブ・マー
リ、ブラックサバス、モット・ザ・フープルなど、過去
の大ヒットアルバムがここでレコーディングされた。

　1975年にベイジング・ストリート・スタジオに改
名、1980年代初めにトレバー・ホムとZTTレコード
が引き継いで、サームウエストと改名し、1984年には
世界的に大ヒットとなったエチオピア救済のため結
成されたスーパーグループ、バンドエイドの『ドゥ・ゼ
イ・ノウ・イッツ・クリスマス？ 』がここの第一スタジ
オで収録され、たくさんの有名歌手たちが、その歌声
を録音するためにここに立ち寄ったのである。

　残念なことに、ここもほかの録音スタジオと同じ
く、レコーディング用施設のままよりも高級マンショ

ンに建て直したほうが物件の価値が上がるという判断により、2014年に閉鎖されてしまった。

All Saints Road（オールセイント通り）はビートルズマニアたちが出てくるシーンのロケ地である。1964年映画『ハード・デイス・ナイト(邦題：ビートルズがやってくるヤア！ヤア！ヤア！)』のためにあの４人組がやってきて「歓声を上げ追いかけてくる女の子のファンから逃げてきたリンゴ・スターが、古道具屋(No.20)に避難する」シーンの撮影を行った。

　ポートベロ通りを北に行くと大きなコンクリートの高速道路が頭上に配した **Westway flyover**（ウェストウェイ高架道路)がある。現在高架下にはお店や喫茶店ができているが、道路ができたばかりの1970年初頭にさかのぼると、ここはまさしく無人地帯、整地が終わったばかりのだだっ広い空き地で　路上ライブの会場として使うことが流行っていた。よく演奏に来ていたのはホークウィンドで、彼らは即席のステージで、無料ライブをしていた。もしラッドブローク・グローブからノッティングヒルの「ご当地バンド」を上げるとしたら、やはりホークウィンドだろうか。

　ポートベロ通りをさらに北向きに歩き**No.307**は1970年代にアングラ出版の主要格、元フレンズ雑誌社の本拠地があったところだ。1969年12月に、もともとは『Frendz of Rolling Stone（フレンズ・オブ・ローリング・ストーンズ)』という名で初刊が発行された。1970年に、『OZ（オズマガジン)』、『IT　（イン

ターナショナルタイムス)』と一緒に『Frendz（フレンズ）』として再刊行され、出版業者のオルタナティブ雑誌革命の先駆けとなった。いずれの雑誌も難しい内容に果敢に挑み、新しいグラフィック・デザインを生み出した。

　ロックミュージック専門の写真家の草分け的存在、ペニー・スミスの初期の作品もふんだんに使われた。彼女が撮影した有名なロックミュージシャンの写真には、レッド・ツェッペリン、U2、ザ・ストーン・ローゼズなどの名が連なる。誌上でよくコンビを組んだジャーナリストのニック・ケントもまた1970年代を代表する重要なロックミュージック専門の評論家であった。

　ラッドブロック・グローブに向かい、**Elgin Pub**（エルギン・パブ）**96 Ladbroke Grove**、ここもまたノッティングヒルの人気施設で、ここで酒を飲んだり演奏したりしていた地元の伝説的パンクバンド、ザ・クラッシュの逸話に出てくる重要スポットである。1975年エルギンは、ジョー・ストラマーのバンド　101ers（ワンハンドレッド・ワナーズ）に9か月間にわたる週末ライブ演奏を依頼した。エルギンの新しいマネージャー、バーニー・ロードスがギタリストのミック・ジョーンズに歌手のジョー・ストラマーとベイシストのポール・シムノンを引き合わせたその翌年の1976年の春、ザ・クラッシュが結成され、その秋にはC3Sレコードと契約を結んだ。最も有名なシングル『ホワイト・ライオット（邦題：白い暴動）』は1976年のノッティングヒル・カーニバル暴動から生まれた曲であ

る。

　彼らはどんなに有名になっても自分たちのルーツがどこにあるのかを忘れることはなく、1979年発表されたアルバム『ロンドン・コーリング』の発表を記念して、ウェストウェイ高架下のアックラム・ホール（現存しない）で2回の無料クリスマスコンサートを行い、地元のファンに感謝の意を表した。

　ラッドブローク・グローブをさらに南に **Blenheim Crescent**（ベルネム・クレセント）で右に曲がって**No.57**の屋根裏部屋の窓を見てみよう。ここは、1968年マーク・ボランが『ライド・ア・ホワイトスワン』をギター片手に作曲し、元ティラノサウルス・レックスのボンゴ演奏者のスティーブ・ペレグリン・トックと一緒にセッションしていた場所である。長髪で美しい顔立ちのボランは、ジョンズ・チルドレンのころの子供っぽいモッズスタイルを卒業すると、煙をふかして詩人のシェリルと小説家トールキンの話をするような、典型的なヒッピースタイルを確立した。

　ベルネム・クレセントをそのまま東にラッドブローク通りをわたってポートベロ通りに向かう途中の右手に、秘密の道のような **Codrington Mews**（コリントン・ミュー）の入り口がある。このあたりのミューの多くは、車が発明される前、馬用の厩舎が必要だったころのものだ。通りから少し入ったところに位置し、厩舎扉をそのまま残して、騒音の都会の中の閑寂の空間となっている。

　コリントン・ミューの1と1Aの壁には、大きなモ

Stanley Donwood's Mural
（スタンリー・ドンウッドの壁画）

ノクロの壁画があり、そこにはロンドンのランドマークが竜巻のようなうねりで吹き消されている様子が描かれている。これはグラフィックデザイナーのスタンリー・ドンウッドの『ロンドンの景色』という作品で、1989年XL（エックス・エル）レコーディングスという名前で創設されたレコード会社の本社の壁に、リチャード・ラッセルがコミッションしたものである。XLレコーディングはデジタル時代が押し寄せる中に唯一生き残っているレコード会社の一つで、アデル、ザ・ホワイトストライプ、レディオヘッドなどでレコードの売り上げを伸ばしている。

　このウォーキングの終点をめざして、ラッドブロック・グローブに戻り、少し南に歩くと、永遠のギターヒーロー、ジミ・ヘンドリックスに敬意の念を抱くファンの巡礼地になっている場所がある。彼が**No.22**

Lansdowne Crescent （ランズドウン・クレセント）
で亡くなったのは1970年9月18日、当時ここは、サマル
カンド・ホテルであった。9月17日、ジミはご機嫌な様
子で、ガールフレンドのモニカ・ダンネマンを連れて
507号室にチェックインし、ホテルの外庭で笑いなが
らお茶を飲み、そのあと、近くのおしゃれなケンジン
トン・マーケットに買い物に出かけた。靴と皮のコー
トを買った彼は、そこで元恋人だったキャシー・エッ
チングハムとばったり会うのだが、それは2人が顔を
合わせる最後となってしまった。

　その夜に起こった出来事の所見は様々であるもの
の、胃の中に大量の睡眠薬と赤ワインが混ざってい
たという検証の結果より、ジミは翌早朝に吐き気を催
し、それが喉に詰まって窒息死したとみられている。
ザ・アニマルズのリードシンガーのエリック・バードン
がベッド横に「僕の生涯」と書かれた遺書のような走
り書きを見つけたことで、最初の発見現場では自殺の
可能性も疑われたが、その後このメモは彼が亡くなる
直前に作っていた歌詞の一部あると認定された。

　ジミ・ヘンドリックスにかかわる住所はここだけで
ない。1967年に彼が一時住んでいた167番地ウエス
トボーン・グローブの家は当時外壁が紫色に塗られ
ていた。それが彼のシングル『パープル・ヘイズ（邦
題：紫の紫煙）』のもとになったのではないかといわ
れている。

－ 建物・人物・場所 －

N

1, トニー・ベンの家 Tony Benn's home, 12 Holland Park Avenue.
2, アヴォンデール公園 Avondale Park. 3, スペイン戦争の壁画
Spanish Civil War mural. 4, スペイン学校 The Spanish School,
317-318 Portbello Road. 5, ガルシア Garcia, 248-250 Portobello
Road. 6, リスボア・カフェ Café Lisboa, 57 Golborne Road.

のウォーキングコースではノッティングヒルの特筆すべき建物とその建物に住んでいた人たち、そして多様な階級、民族、文化が共存するノッティングヒルを形作る重要な役目をした場所をご紹介する。

Notting Hill Gate（ノッティングヒル・ゲート）からスタートして、**Holland Park Avenue**（ホランドパーク・アベニュー）を西に向かって歩いてみよう。この道はロンドン最古の街道のひとつで、ローマ帝国がイギリス本土を支配していた時代（BC55年〜410年）、ローマ軍がイノシシやシカのいる深い森を切り開いて作った直線道である。その後オックスフォードとロンドンを結ぶ主要国道となり、現在もこの道には<u>オックスフォード・チューブ</u>と呼ばれる、ロンドンとオックスフォードを結ぶ直行バスサービスが運行している。中世期（1200〜）になると森は少しずつ切り開かれ、現在のノッティングヒル・ゲート駅付近に少しずつ集落のようなものができ始めたが、この道の追いはぎや野盗の被害は後を絶たず、道路は荒れ放題、一部通行すら難しいという無法状態が18世紀まで続いた。1714年の議会で、道路保全を目的にした通行料を徴収することを容認する決議が採択されたので、通行料取立て門（ターンパイク）がノッティングヒル・ゲートに建てられ1860年代まで通行料徴収による道路管理がなされた。

No.12 Holland Park Avenue（ホランドパーク・アベニュー）、ここは1980年代の半ばにノッティングヒルで僕が初めての訪れた住所だ。ベテランの労働党議

Labour MP Tony Benn's former home
労働党故トニー・ベンの家

員のトニー・ベンが奥さんのキャロラインと1952年から2014年まで住んでいた。ベン家族は僕の親戚だったので、家族でロンドンに行くときは必ずこの家に立ち寄って、居心地のいいリビングルームでお茶をのんだ。パイプを片手にトニーは妹と僕に学校のことや

ロンドンでの予定を聞いたりした。奥さんのキャロライン・デキャンプ・ベンは2000年に他界したが、彼女の教育に対する偉業をたたえるプラークがその家の壁にかけられている。彼女はコンプリヘンシブ教育推進運動（注*）の共同発足者で、ベン家の子供たちが通った近くのホランドパーク・コンプリヘンシブ運営と推進に尽力した。

（注*：Comprehensive Education　無選抜の地域密接型中等教育。すべての子供が平等に教育を受けられるようにという労働党の方針に元づいて推進された）

　ホランドパーク・アベニューを西向きに歩き次の交差点を右に入ると、そこは丘のように盛り上がった**Ladbroke Grove**（ラッドブローク・グローブ）の南端にあたる。このあたりが17世紀には農地だったと想像するのはちょっと難しいかもしれない。変化が訪れるのは1829年、地主ジェームス・ウェラー＝ラッドブロークがこの土地を祖父母から譲り受けた時に、この地域を一変する壮大な土地改革に乗り出し、それから25年以上の年月をかけてその区画は変貌を遂げるのである。1823年、もっとも信頼を寄せていた建築家のトーマス・オラソンに彼が依頼したのは、メイフェアやベルグレイブに対抗する新興住宅地の区画設計図を描くことであった。オラソンは公共の公園か庭に囲まれ、道が南北に通り、2つの大きな住宅地のアイデアを提案した。（それがのちのラッドブローク・グローブになる）。建設工事はすぐに始まったが、"1825年の恐慌"と呼ばれる金融危機で労働者

は職を失い、その後17年もの間、その事業は中断を
余儀なくされた。

　ノッティングヒルには合計16か所のガーデンス
クエアと呼ばれる庭園広場があることで有名だ
が、**Ladbroke Square and Ladbroke Grove**（ラッドグ
ローブ・スクエアとラッドブローク・グローブ）の交
差点に立つと、その一つが見える。そこはプライベー
トの共用庭園で、運よく庭園が裏ぐちとつながって
いる家に住んでいる裕福な住民だけしか使用でき
ない。『ノッティングヒルの恋人』の映画に出てきた
ヒュー・グラントとジュリア・ロバーツがロマンティ
ックな夜を過ごした庭園は、ここから北に向かって
いくつかの交差点を渡ったところにある **Rosemead
Gardens**（ローズミード・ガーデン）である。

　ラッドブローク・グローブをさらに北向きに歩いて
Lansdowne Crescent（ランズドウン・クレセント）に
入ると、ここはちょうど1830年代に数年だけつくられ
た競馬場の中央部分にあたる。1837年、ウェラー＝
ラッドブローク氏の建設工事が延期になったことを
知った地元の実業家ジェームス・ウェイトが、アスコ
ットやエプソムに対抗すべく、ケンジントン・ヒポド
ロムと名打った競馬場を作ることを提案した。ジェー
ムスは140エーカー（東京ドーム約12個分）の土地の
借り、意気揚々とコース周りに高い木塀を立て始め
た。それが悪かった。一部の住民たち、特に **Pottery
Lane**（ポトリー・レーン）、別名「魔の小道」に住む、
生きるためには手段を択ばない超貧困にあえぐ住民
たちの反感を買ってしまったのだ。その塀は公共の

権利道路(誰でも通行可能な私有道)を横切る形で
建てられたので、当然スラム住民の通り道は所々で
寸断されてしまい、競馬の開催日には、ウェイトが顧
客として想定していなかった、小汚いスラムの住人達
が塀の内側に現れて競技が中断された。度重なる住
民との問題に加えて、柔らかい粘土質の土壌は競馬
場にはまったく適さないということも判明した。水は
けが悪くすぐにぬかるんでしまう土壌では、騎手たち
も安全性を理由にそのレース場で馬に乗るのを拒否
するようになったのである。結局1837年から1842年
までの間に開催した競馬レースはたった13回。事業
の失敗を認めたウェイトは、地主に土地を返却した。
その後住宅建設は再開され、長期にわたる建築工事
が終了したのである。

　西に向かって，**Lansdowne Rise**（ロンズドウン・
ライズ）→ **Clarendon Road**（クレンドン通り）→
Hippodrome Place（ヒポドローム・プレース）→
Walmer Road（ワルマー通り）、かつては貧困地域だ
ったこの地域では、今メガベイスメント増改築が盛ん
に行われている。家の地下に、室内プール、シネマ、
ワインセラー、ジム、駐車場などを作るというもの
で、チェルシー・ケンジントン区役所によれば、通称
アイスバーグ・ハウスと呼ばれるそのような家の建築
認可申請の件数は、2001年の13件から、2016年には
200件に跳ね上がったという。ドリルで地下を掘り起
こし、玄関の庭に設置されたベルトコンベアで土砂
を運び出し、それを運ぶ大型トラックが頻繁に行き
来する工事現場は騒音振動や粉塵公害が深刻な問

Kiln　（キルム・窯）

題になっている。しかも工事が終了するまでには平
均2年くらいの年月がかかり、近所同士の建築紛争が

絶えないようだ。

Walmer Road（ワルマー通り）は、かつてロンドン
でも最も貧困だった地域のど真ん中である。そこで
は2つの生業、養豚とレンガ作りが人々の生活の糧で
あった。住人以外は足を踏み入れることすらなかっ
た地域だったが、チャールズディケンズは1850年にこ
う記している。「…その不潔さによる疫病の斑点は、
ほかのロンドンの地区と比べ物にならない…」。

ワルマー通りには煉瓦（レンガ）を加工するのに
つかわれた最後のキルム（窯）があり建築用煉瓦が
つくられていた。ちょうど建築業が急成長していた
ので、ロンドンの中心部から郊外で煉瓦の需要も伸
びていた。煉瓦工はトットナムコートからマーブルア
ーチが都心化するに従い、西のほうに追いやられ、
結果的に養豚業者と隣り合わせで暮らすようになっ
ていた。スラム地区の住環境は悪化する一方だ。役
所の都市計画もなく、上水道もきちんとした下水処
理もない。豚と人の排せつ物が一緒に粘土を掘り出
した穴に投棄された。ちょうどキルム（窯）の前にあ
る **Avondale Park**（アヴォンデール公園）は、この辺
りで一番大きな採掘穴で、「ザ・オーシャン（大海原）
」と呼ばれていたが、1892年に埋め立てられて、現在
は緑地公園となっている。家の価格が億単位で売買
されるようになった今、裕福にしか見えないこの地域
に、かつて究極の貧困生活が存在したことを想像す
るのは難しい。

St Andrew's Square（セント・アンドリュー・ス
クエア）には、かつて **No.10 Rillington Place**（リリン

トン・プレイス）という住所が存在した。おそらくこ
の地域で最も不名誉な住所だっただろう。1943年8
月から1953年3月まで、ここにジョン・レジナルド・ク
リスティという男が住んでいた。8人の女性を殺害し、
それらの死体を床板の下と小さな裏庭に埋めて隠し
た殺人魔である。しかしその犯罪の全貌が明らかに
なったのは、クリスティがその家を引き払った1953年
であった。それは奇しくも同じ家の2階に住んでいた
ティモシー・エバンスが、自分の妻と子供を殺害した
という罪（実際はクリスティの犯行の冤罪）で首つり
処刑されてから3年経った後のことであった。

　ゆがんだ人格を隠し、地元に貢献する人物だとい
う印象を与えることに巧みだったクリスティは、戦時
中には予備警察軍に雇われるほどだった。また、自
分には医療知識があると吹聴し、地元の喫茶店やケ
ンジントンパーク・ホテル（今のＫＨＰパブ）などの
飲み屋で売春婦を捕まえては、リリントン・プレイス
に連れ帰り、ガス毒殺か絞殺をした。1953年3月その
家の2階に住んでいたベレスフォード・ブラウンが、台
所の壁に隠されたアルコーブに最後の被害者女性3
人の死体を発見、それを受けて警察の一斉捜索が開
始された。プトニー・ブリッジ近くのエンバンクメント
で、クリスティは警察に身柄を拘束された。3月31日の
ことだった。6月の公判でクリスティはすべての殺人
の罪を認め、その上で自分は精神異常だと訴えたが、
これは審判員に却下され、有罪判決が下された。そ
してその一か月後、ペントンビル刑務所で首つり処刑
となったのだ。

　この陰惨な実話の最終章は、ティモシー・エバンスの冤罪を描いたベストセラー『10 Rillington Place（リリントン・プレイス）』の原作者ルドビック・ケネディが脚本を描き下ろし、リチャード・アッテンボロ主演で1971年に『10 Rillington Place（邦題：10番街の殺人）』として映画化された。そのロケには、まさしくその殺人現場、リリントン・プレイスの家が使われたのである。1970年に映画の収録が終わると同時に、ウェストウェイ高速道路用地にするという名目もあり解体業者がその通りにも入った。その家はそういった解体作業員たちの手によって斧とかまでゆっくりとはぎとられるように取り壊されたのだった。

　ランカスター通りを歩いてラッドブローク通りを北に向かい、**Westway flyover**（ウェストウェイ高架道路）まで来たら東に向きにポートベロ通りまで歩こう。巨大なコンクリートの柱で支えられたちょうどパディントン駅にまで続く電車の線路の頭上に並行に並ぶ自動車道の建設は、当初シェパーズ・ブッシュ付近の交通渋滞を緩和するという目的で計画された。工事は1964年に始まり1970年終了、ヨーロッパで一番長い高架バイパスの完成と称された。実際ロンドン市内の交通緩和と車での移動時間の短縮が約束された有意義な工事ではあったものの、貧しい地域住民の生活は無視され、工事によって多大な迷惑と混乱を強いられることになった。地元住民の強い反対運動の甲斐もなく工事は認可されてしまったが、自動車道がオープンすると、1か月するかしないうちに1日に47000台もの車がノッティングヒルの上空を通過

するという早速の成果を得た。その自動車道の高架
下の土地は現在ウェストウェイ・トラストによって管
理され、金曜日と土曜日の蚤の市のときは、うるさい
自動車道が頭上にあるなんてことも、みんな忘れて
しまうようだ。

　ポートベロ通りに着いたら、まず見てほしいのが電
車の陸橋の下の壁を飾っているカラフルなモザイク
壁画である。それは1936年から39年にかけてのスペ
インの市民戦争の時に、ケンジントンから派遣され
た国際旅団義勇軍の有志をたたえて2006年に進呈
されたものだ。そしてこのあたりは歴史的にもスペイ
ン人コミュニティの中心である。1930年代のスペイン
市民戦争の時、フランコ総督の圧力政治に耐えかね
た多くの移民がこの地域に流れ込み、1970年代に第
二期の移民の波がそこに合流した。壁画から北に少
し歩くと、その時に建てられた **The Spanish school**
（スペイン学校）**317–318 Portobello Road**があ
る。高いブロック塀に囲まれて中を見ることはできな
いが、その学校は現在もスペイン政府によって運営
されており、ノッティングヒルのスペイン人コミュニテ
ィの柱になっている。

　またおすすめのスペイン食材店、**Garcia**（ガル
シア）**248-250 Portobello Road** も付け加えておこ
う。ガルシア食材店はマラガ島出身の家族が1957年
創業以来ずっと経営している老舗である。

Golborne Road（ゴルボーン通り)に到着。ゴルボ
ーンはこの10年の間に、高級ブティックやらおしゃれ
なカフェが立ち並び、ずいぶん綺麗になったが、ボヘ

139

ミアンな雰囲気も健在するポートベロ通りの妹分というところだろうか。金曜日と土曜日にはこの通りにも蚤の市屋台が立ち、にわかに活気が出る。特に古い家具や食器類の古道具に特化していて掘り出し物がいっぱいだ。

ここで**No.92**の一見なんともぱっとしない建物のことを一筆しておこう。これは1864年に建てられた、ピーケ・ハウスという名で知られている建物で、1980年代までは教会だった。

1990年代、しばらく所有者のない空き家だったので、不法侵入者に占拠されていた時期もあったが、ファッションデザイナーでビートルズのポール（マッカートニー）の娘、ステラ・マッカートニーが買い取り、2003年以降は彼女のロンドン本社になった。

Café Lisboa（リスボア・カフェ）**57 Golborne Road**でコーヒーとポルトガルのおいしいお菓子パティス・デ・ナタを注文し、表通りのテーブル席に座ると、頭上に **Trellick Tower**（テレリック・タワー）が見えるだろう。1966年ロンドン市役所がモダニスト建築の名手、エルノ・ゴールドフィンガーにデザイン委託したこのテレリック・タワーは1972年に完成、98メーターの高さがあり、同時期に西ロンドン地区のポプラーに建てられた、同氏設計のバルフロン・タワーより若干小さいが同じデザインの建物だ。特徴のあるサービス・タワーが建物の横に作られて、3階ごとに通路でつながっている。その建物に対しては意見が二つに割れた。素晴らしいモダン建築の代表的な見本だという意見と、見た目に不細工で暗いという意見だ。ジ

Trellick Tower（テレリック・タワー）

ェームス・ボンドの脚本作家、イアン・フレミングはモ
ダニズム建築特にゴールドフィンガーの作品を毛嫌
いしていたので、彼の名前を自作の悪役に使ったと言

っている。ゴールドフィンガーは当初コンシェルジェ
（受付管理）システムを導入し居住者を委員会で選考
する提案をしていたが、それは役所に却下された。
完成のころまでには、高層集合住宅には社会的問題
（犯罪の巣窟）が絡むため、「空に向かって伸びる住
宅街」というモダニズム建築の盛大な思想はもはや
賛美されるものではなくなってしまった。1970年代以
降1980年全般に、テレリック・タワーには麻薬と暴力
の温床というレッテルが張られた。1980年代半ばく
らいになってようやくコンシェルジェとインター・コ
ムのシステムが導入され、化粧直しをした公共住宅
の大部分、217戸のが、憧れの住所として、個人向け
に不動産売買された。

　テレリック・タワーは歌や書籍、映画にも時折出て
くる。ＪＧ（ジェームス・グレア）・バラードの反ユート
ピア小説『ハイ・ライズ』、マーティン・アミスの小説『
ロンドン・フィールド』、そしてブラーの曲『ベスト・デ
イズ』などである。

– 追記 –

2017年7月14日、グレンフェル・タワーで大規模な火災が発生した。これはもう一つのブルータリスト建築（*注）の公共団地であった。古いコンクリート打放し外観を目隠しするために、近年施工された可燃性の高い外壁材と、スプリンクラーの欠如によって、火災は瞬く間に上階まで広がってしまった。たった一つしかない屋内の避難階段は、上層階の住人達の逃げ道にはならず、その結果、71人が死亡、多くの貧困住民が家を失ったのである。（*注：Brutalismコンクリートの打放しなど直接的な素材の使い方を志向する現代建築様式）

　地元民ボランティアは救援に乗り出し、炊き出しが行われた。たくさんの衣服や寝具が寄せられ、キリスト教会、イスラム教モスク、そしてあらゆる宗教施設が緊急の住まいとして被害者に提供された。ノッティングヒル・カーニバルはその年、「Green for Grenfell（グリーン・フォー・グレンフェル）」を掲げ、被害者の冥福を祈るために、テレリック・タワーを含むいくつかのロンドンの建物が緑色に点灯されたのである。

　テレリック・タワーのグラフィティ・ゾーンにはたくさんの絵が描かれ、人々の悲嘆と失望と怒りが表現されている。ストームジーをはじめとする多くのアーティストに支持されて立ち上がったグレンフェル問責

抗議運動は、被害者の人権、同様の公共住宅に対す
る安全の確保を強く訴えている。

– 索引 –

HOSTELS

ボウデン・コート・ホステル
Bowden Court
24 Ladbroke Road W11 3NN
0203 740 2429
www.lhalondon.com/bowden-court/

レンスター・ホステル
The Leinster Hostel
44–46 Leinster Gardens W2 3AT
0203 740 9845
www.lhalondon.com/leinster-house

ENTERTAINMENT

アックラム・ビレッジ・マーケット（屋台村・イベント）
Acklam Village Market
4–8 Acklam Road W10 5TY
www.acklamvillage.com

エレクトリック・シネマ　　（映画館）
The Electric Cinema
191 Portobello Road, Notting Hill W11 2ED
0207 908 9696
www.electriccinema.co.uk/portobello

ゲートシアター（劇場）
The Gate Theatre
11 Pembridge Road W11 3HQ
0207 229 0706
www.gatetheatre.co.uk

ノッティングヒル・アートクラブ (ナイトクラブ)
Notting Hill Arts Club
21 Notting Hill Gate W113JQ
0207 460 4459
www.nottinghillartsclub.com

プリントルーム (旧コロネット劇場)
The Print Room at the Coronet
103 Notting Hill Gate W11 3LB
0203 642 6606 (box office)
www.the-print-room.org

ターバナックル　　　(アート・センター)
Tabernacle
35 Powis Square, off Portobello Road W11 2AY
www.tabernaclew11.com

BOOKSHOPS

ブックス・フォー・クックス (料理本)
Books for Cooks
4 Blenheim Crescent W11 1NN
0207 221 1992
www.booksforcooks.com

ブック&コミック・エクスチェンジ (古本)
Book & Comic Exchange
30 & 32 Pembridge Road W11 3HN
0207 598 2233

ダウント・ブックス
Daunt Books
112–14 Holland Park Avenue W11 4UA
0207 727 7022
www.dauntbooks.co.uk/holland-park/

ルティエンス＆ルビンスタイン・ブックショップ
Lutyens & Rubinstein Bookshop
21 Kensington Park Road W11 2EU
0207 229 1010
www.lutyensrubinstein/bookshop/

ノッティングヒル・ブックショップ
The Notting Hill Bookshop
13 Blenheim Crescent W11 2EE
0207 229 5260
www.thenottinghillbookshop.co.uk

SHOPS

281番地　ポートベロ・ロード（雑貨）
281 Portobello Road
281 Portobello Road W10 5TZ
0208 960 2277
www.281portobelloroad.com

イソップ（化粧品）
Aesop
61 Golborne Road W10 5NR
0208 964 9731
westbourne@aesop.com

エージェント・プロヴォケーター (ランジェリー)
Agent Provocateur
303 Westbourne Grove W11 2QA
0207 243 1292
www.agentprovocateur.com

アリスのアンティーク (骨董品)
Alice's Antiques
86 Portobello Rd W11 2QD
0207 229 8187

アリー・カペリーノ (ファッション)
Ally Capellino
312 Portobello Road W10 5RU
0208 964 1022
www.allycapellino.co.uk

アンティーク・クロージング・ショップ (古着)
The Antique Clothing Shop
282 Portobello Road W10 5TE
0208 964 4830
www.282portobello.london

アーミー・クラッシックス (古着・軍服)
Army Classics
49 Pembridge Road W11 3HG
0207 221 7117

バーム・アンティーク (骨董品)
Barham Antiques
83 Portobello Road W11 2QB

0207 727 3845
www.barhamantiques.co.uk

クーベルチュール＆ザ・ガーブストア（ファッション）
Couverture & The Garbstore
188 Kensington Park Road W11 2ES
0207 229 2178
www.couvertureandthegarbstore.com

グラハム＆グリーン（雑貨）
Graham & Green
4 Elgin Crescent W11 2HX
0207 243 8908
www.grahamandgreen.co.uk

オネスト・ジョン（レコード）
Honest Jon's
278 Portobello Road W10 5TE
0208 969 9822
www.honestjons.com

クレアントス・アンティーク（骨董品）
Kleanthous Antiques
144 Portobello Road W11 2DZ
0207 727 3649
www.kleanthous.com

リンドンズ・アート＆グラフィック（画材）
Lyndons Art and Graphics
Unit 1, 216 Kensington Park Rd W11 1NR
0207 727 5192

オックスファム（チャリティー・ショップ）
Oxfam Shop
144 Notting Hill Gate W11 3QG
0207 792 0037

ポール・スミス（ファッション）
Paul Smith
Westbourne House
122 Kensington Park Road W11 2EP
0207 727 3553
www.paulsmith.com

ペドラーの雑貨店とカフェ（雑貨）
Pedlars General Store and Café
128 Talbot Road, Notting Hill W11 1JA
0207 727 7799
www.pedlars.co.uk

レリック（古着）
Rellik
8 Golborne Rd W10 5NW
0208 962 0089
www.relliklondon.co.uk.

ラフ・トレード（レコード）
Rough Trade
130 Talbot Road W11 1JA
0207 229 8541
www.roughtrade.com

シーラクック・テキスタイル（古着・布）
Sheila Cook Textiles
26 Addison Place W11 4RJ
0207 603 3003
www.sheilacook.co.uk

スパイス・ショップ（食品）
The Spice Shop
1 Blenheim Crescent W11 2EE
0207 221 4448
www.thespiceshop.co.uk

サブ・クチュール（ファッション）
Sub Couture
204 Kensington Park Road W11 1NR
0207 229 5434
www.subcouture.co.uk

スープラ（ファッション）
Supra
249 Portobello Road W11 1LT
0207 243 3130
www.supralondon.com

和装館（和装小物）
Wasoukan
293 Westbourne Grove W11 2QA
0203 637 5010
www.wasoukan.eu

ワイルド・アット・ハート (生花)
Wild at Heart
222 Westbourne Grove W11 2RH
0207 727 3095
www.wildatheart.com

RESTAURANTS/PUBS

ビーチ・ブランケット・バビロン (レストラン・バー)
Beach Blanket Babylon
45 Ledbury Road W11 2AA
0207 229 2907
www.beachblanket.co.uk

クラークのレストラン
Clarke's Restaurant
124 Kensington Church Street W8 4BH
0207 221 9225
www.sallyclarke.com

コットン　(カリブ料理)
Cottons
157–9 Notting Hill Gate W11 3LF
0207 243 0090
www.cottons-restaurant.co.uk

ザ・カウ　(英国・創作料理)
The Cow
89 Westbourne Park W2 5QH
0207 221 5400 or 0207 221 0021
www.thecowlondon.co.uk

ダ・マリア　（イタリア料理）
Da Maria
87b Notting Hill Gate W11 3JZ
0207 792 4491
www.damaria.co.uk

ディスティリリー　（パブ）
The Distillery
186 Portobello Road W11 1LA
0203 034 2233
www.the-distillery.london

エルギン　（パブ）
The Elgin
96 Ladbroke Grove W11 1PY
0207 229 5663
www.theelginnottinghill.co.uk

ジールス　（レストラン・バー）
Geales
2 Farmer St W8 7SN
0207 727 7528
www.geales.com

ケンジントン・プレイス　（魚介料理）
Kensington Place
201 Kensington Church St W8 7LX
0207 727 3184
www.kensingtonplace-restaurant.co.uk

トレイラー・ハピネス　（バー＆ライブ音楽）
Trailer Happiness
177 Portobello Road W11 2DY
trailerh.com

アクスブリッジ・アームズ　（パブ）
Uxbridge Arms
13 Uxbridge Street W8 7TQ
Tel 0207 792 1362
www.theuxbridgearmskensington.co.uk

CAFÉ/TAKE AWAY

リスボア・カフェ　（ベーカリー＆カフェ）
Café Lisboa
57 Golborne Road W10 5NR
0208 968 5242
www.cafelisboa.co.uk

コーヒー・プラント　（豆焙煎・カフェ）
The Coffee Plant
180 Portobello Road W11 2EB
0207 221 8137
www.coffee.uk.com

ジョージ・フィッシュ・バー　（フィッシュ＆チップス）
George's Portobello Fish Bar
329 Portobello Road W10 5SA
0208 969 7895

グレイン・ショップ　（ベジタリアン・デリ&カフェ）
The Grain Shop
269A Portobello Rd W11 1LR
0207 229 5571

マイクのカフェ　（イングリッシュ・ブレックファースト）
Mike's Café
12 Blenheim Cresc W11 1NN
0207 229 3757

ミスター・クリスチャン・リミテッド (デリ)
Mr Christian's Limited
43 Portland Rd W11 4LJ
0207 229 0501
www.mrchristians.co.uk